YOUR ADULT B-MITZVAH

A Guide From Those Who Have Gone Before

Christine Machlin

Ben Yehuda Press
Teaneck, New Jersey

Published by Ben Yehuda Press
122 Ayers Court #1B
Teaneck, NJ 07666

http://www.BenYehudaPress.com

Ben Yehuda Press books may be purchased for educational, business or sales promotional use.
information, please contact:
Special Markets, Ben Yehuda Press,
122 Ayers Court #1B, Teaneck, NJ 07666
markets@BenYehudaPress.com

Permissions and Acknowledgements:

ISBN13 978-1-934730-76-8

19 20 21/ 10 9 8 7 6 5 4 3 2 1   20251011

To Robert

My husband, My Best Friend, and My Bashert

For my dad

*Whose belief in me never wavered
and gave me the courage to chase every dream.*

Contents

Introduction   1

My Story   5
Deciding This Is for You   9
Hebrew: "Lots of Dots"   14
The Not-So-Terrifying Trope   18
Your Torah Portion   23
Hear Ye, Hear Ye! Writing Your D var Torah   27
Writing Your Jewish Journey Speech   33
Prepping for the Bimah   38
The Big Day   43
So What Happens Now?   53

Student Stories   56

Acknowledgements   169
Glossary   172
Resources   176

Introduction

Shalom!

If you're anything like me then you've picked up this book for one very important reason: you are about to embark or are considering embarking on the very exciting and rewarding journey that is the adult Bar/Bat Mitzvah. Let me tell you that even the choice to go through this process is a mitzvah of its own. You should be very proud of yourself for getting to this point, because for most people it is not easy. It can be scary and intimidating. Some of you might take this journey alone, but I'm here to tell you that you are most definitely *not* alone.

My intention in writing this is to provide some background education and steps through the process, and to let you know what you might expect in your journey to the Torah. I've also collected personal accounts from students across the United States, ranging in age from late thirties to early nineties. Their stories tell the tale of someone who was once just like you—someone who had always wanted to become a Bar/Bat Mitzvah but did not for whatever reason. So, what did they do? Just like you, they, too, decided that it was the time to take that next step, to commit their time and effort to study Hebrew and be called to the Torah, and boy were they glad they did!

Now it's your turn! I'd like this book to serve as your companion in your current (or future) B-Mitzvah class (I'm going to use *B-Mitzvah* to encompass both Bar and Bat Mitzvah for the sake of brevity throughout the book). Sometimes opening the Hebrew textbook can be intimidating. Every week you learn new words and phrases when you haven't mastered the ones you learned last week, or the week before that! To some, this can be overwhelming, discouraging, and ultimately frustrating. When that happens, I want you to reach for this book and reread some of the chapters and stories of former students. I encourage you to highlight, dog-ear the pages, and write notes in the margins. When the moments come (and they will) where you feel like giving up, go to those chapters or stories that you have saved and read them until you've found that encouragement you were lacking. That is my ultimate wish for you!

For those who have converted to Judaism, or non-Jewish family/ friends reading this in support of someone, you might ask, *What is a B-Mitzvah exactly? Where and when did this ritual get started, and what is its purpose?* Great questions!

It began with the Bar Mitzvah. Bar Mitzvah is Aramaic for "Son of the Commandment," and while the ritual of *Bar* Mitzvah has been around since the second century CE, *B-Mitzvah* was not formally introduced until the early twentieth century. It was then that the Bar Mitzvah finally got is companion, the *Bat* Mitzvah. On March 18, 1922, Judith Kaplan, daughter of Reconstructionist Movement Founder Rabbi Mordecai Kaplan, became the first Bat Mitzvah in America at age 13. Though this was a momentous occasion in Jewish history, the practice of *Bat* Mitzvah was not common until the 1970s—but she certainly paved the way to this wonderful tradition! This led to calling the ceremony B'nai Mitzvah, which is the plural that can include both genders, or the more inclusive Bar or Bat Mitzvah.

When a boy at age 13, or a girl at age 12, becomes a B-Mitzvah, they take on a huge responsibility to live a moral and religious life. At this point in their lives, the consequences of their actions are their responsibility. A B-Mitzvah can join a minyan, receive an aliyah, and can chant from the Torah.

Girls and women outside of Orthodox Judaism now have equal religious rights and obligations as boys and men. B'nai Mitzvah can now chant from the Torah and lead religious services. It's a great time to be alive, isn't it?

And now, even though you're past 12 or 13, maybe it's your turn!

You're never too old for an adult B-Mitzvah!

Today, many synagogues provide the opportunity to become a B-Mitzvah to people who were not able to celebrate this ritual when they were younger. Reasons can vary, such as conversion to Judaism as an adult; men who were born Jewish but were not encouraged by their families to undergo the process; or women who grew up before it was common for females to become a Bat Mitzvah.

Unfortunately, the stereotype that a B-Mitzvah is only for children has created a misconception among many Jews and non-Jews alike that someone going through the process at age 60+ years is ridiculous or even unheard of. So, as a convert with a growing desire to broaden my education and knowledge of my newfound people, I did what any human being living in the twentieth century would do. I did a lot of research before I made a big commitment that would take up a good chunk of time and effort.

As an avid reader, I decided I would try to find some books about the subject of adult B-Mitzvah to help guide me through the process. While I found many online articles about the process, and several websites with information, I could not find books or even educational literature on the *adult* B-Mitzvah! I found educational books for children becoming B-Mitzvah, which I found helpful; but what about me? I am *not* 13. And after reading about programs at various congregations, I knew in my heart that I am *not* alone—and neither are you!

As a recent adult Bat Mitzvah, when I first entered the program, I would casually bring up in conversation, with pride, that I was currently studying Hebrew and would soon be called to the Torah. I had hoped when I spoke with people about this, I would be greeted with support and encouragement. Instead, I got bewilderment, and sometimes questions as to *why* I was doing something that some people viewed as pointless if you aren't a child.

After a few months of soul searching and trying to find someone other than my spouse and my rabbi to give me even an ounce of encouragement and finding nothing, I began to lose hope. I felt alone, I felt empty, and I began to wonder if I was just wasting my time. I am not 13. I am a convert. Why did this *really* matter so much to me?

Unsurprisingly, after several months of complete discouragement, I nearly hit rock bottom and almost decided to drop out of the program before I got ahead of myself. Just before I was completely convinced that maybe this wasn't for me, my research background kicked in to rekindle my desire to pursue this process. I thought to myself, *I couldn't be the only one to feel this way, could I?*

Therefore, I decided to write a book as a modern, *not* 13-year old's guide through the process of the adult B-Mitzvah. Anyone, at any age, can be called to the Torah; just because you missed your calling at 12 or 13 does not mean it's too late for you.

There are hundreds, if not thousands, of people out there who are in your same position and who have become a B-Mitzvah ranging from their early twenties to late eighties. The best part about being a Jew is that it is never too late to begin this journey in life. We are always encouraged at any age to keep learning, keep believing, and keep doing!

My Story

I hope what you find most comforting about this book is hearing the stories of people just like you and me who have been searching to find an even closer connection to their Jewish faith. My journey in Judaism has not been an easy one.

I was born Roman Catholic to two very devout parents. My mother, who I always joke is two rosaries away from being a nun, was the head receptionist at our church's front office and was the confirmation and youth group director. My father was the head usher for all Sunday evening services; played Santa during the church's annual Christmas pancake breakfast; and, like my mother, assisted with teaching confirmation class every year. In my youth, I was quite involved in my Catholic faith and attended many religious retreats and seminars to become an active young adult in the church. I'm not sure what exactly lit a fire inside me, but after my confirmation at the age of 16, where one is truly recognized as an adult in the church, I began to lose my drive and desire to be the best Catholic I could be. Something inside me began to question just why I was there. Was this something I wanted or was this something my parents wanted for me? In my family, I was considered the "good child" when I was younger. I am the youngest of four, with a sister and two older half-brothers; but I never really had that close a relationship with my half-brothers. Due to an unpleasant divorce, my father did not have the best relationship with his younger son, and had an easier time with the older one, who unfortunately passed away in his mid-40s. I spent the most time with my sister, until our relationship deteriorated around the time she started high school; that's when my "good child" reputation started. I never went to any parties (which my sister did quite often); I hated calling in sick for school because I liked going so much (again, not my sister's favorite thing); and all my friends were of the "geek genre," just like me (my sister hung out with the "popular" kids who took great pleasure in tormenting people like my friends and me). Essentially, my parents never really had to worry about me, and with what I have told you, can you really blame them?

The turning point in my reputation as the "good child" hit around the time I stopped going to church with my parents, when I was around 17 or 18, just before I was about to enter college. Attending services with my parents was a ritual I had participated in for as long as I could remember. Every Sunday at 5:30 p.m. I was dressed in my *Sunday Best*, excited and ready for the evening sermon. My parents were not happy when I made the decision to stop going with them. The transition from "Avid Churchgoer" to "Never Churchgoer" started when my parents would ask if I was going to go with them or drive myself, to which I would respond that I wasn't going this week. This happened for several months, until my parents simply stopped asking me. I'm sure they thought, as most parents would, that it was just a phase I was going through and that I would outgrow it. For them, it was only through the Catholic Church that I could rekindle my relationship with Jesus, and therefore I had to be part of the church.

Little did they know how empty I felt inside, like a piece of me was missing. Here I was, this young adult who used to find pleasure and meaning in her faith. Now, I felt as though a part of me had dissipated, which left a wide hole in my heart that I struggled to fill. I felt like a king without a country. That was when I found Judaism.

Initially my dabbling in the Jewish faith simply began by my attending Shabbat services with my friends on Friday night. This happened shortly after I started college. What an odd feeling that was, to be at another religious service that did not recognize Jesus as Lord and Savior as I had believed to be true my entire life. When I attended my first Shabbat service, I was expecting to be greeted by strange looks. I felt people were going to look at me and wonder, *Who is this new girl? Why is she here?* What I experienced was better than I ever could have imagined. When I first set foot in the synagogue, the rabbi greeted me and welcomed me to the congregation. He asked me many questions about myself and really made me feel welcome and in no way a trespasser as I had expected. After speaking with him, I encountered even more members of the congregation who also welcomed me with open arms and smiling faces. It was a powerful and peaceful feeling, and something I will remember for the rest of my life.

Initially, my intention was only to attend a single Shabbat service and then move on to another religious organization until I had found the faith I felt was right for me... but G-d works in mysterious ways. I found myself regularly attending services on Friday nights and soon became an active prospective member of the congregation. I had no idea where this new routine of mine would lead to until one day I was approached by one of my friends who asked me, "Ever thought about actually *becoming* a Jew?" Every aspect of my entire being was called into question at that moment. I was overwhelmed and scared about what a decision like this would mean to me, and how it would affect my relationship with others in my life. But I truly feel when G-d calls you in a direction, as much as you try to deny it and try as hard as you can to pull away, in the end what is meant to be for you will be.

I officially converted to Judaism in June of 2011, at the age of 21, and I have never looked back. I have never felt more at home and alive as when I made the choice to be a Jew, but my journey did not stop there. It was only the beginning.

I recall a conversation with a friend about her cousin's Bar Mitzvah. I told her, "I wish that I was actually *born* Jewish. I would have loved to have had a Bat Mitzvah." She responded, "I think you actually can! My congregation just had their annual adult B-Mitzvah ceremony. It was only a few women, but it was very beautiful."

There it was—the spark of light that I had not felt in a very long time, like something was calling and driving me to learn more. So, I went online and researched whether the synagogue we belonged to had such a program, and to my joy it did! The feeling of being up on the bimah, gazing down at the ancient scroll, and chanting the Hebrew verses in front of people who love you is indescribable. During my Bat Mitzvah it took everything to hold back tears of joy as the congregation, my friends, and my family clapped for me after I was officially announced as a Bat Mitzvah. This was a journey that took two years of my life to achieve. I devoted my time, energy, and social life at times to ensure I was ready for that exact moment. When that moment finally came, it was surreal. All of my study and learning had officially paid off, and the feeling was spectacular.

We will dive further into the process of speaking to your rabbi and signing up for the program in coming chapters. I don't want to give too much away in the beginning! You will also get first-hand accounts of the process, what to expect along the way, and much more. Let this book be your guide through your journey; a "What to Expect When You're Expecting" for the adult B-Mitzvah program. My hope is that if you are reading this book, no matter what stage you are at, you will find much needed guidance and encouragement to stick through it to the very end. Though the journey may be long and trying, close your eyes and picture yourself on the bimah, reading from ancient texts that have been passed down from generation to generation. The journey may be long, but I promise you, it will be worth it!

Deciding This Is for You

So, you've made the decision to begin your journey toward becoming a B-Mitzvah (or you have decided to keep going and not quit). That's a wonderful and exciting first step! But before you start window shopping for a yad (the pointer used when reading from the Torah) and a tallit (the prayer shawl), take this opportunity to mentally prepare yourself for how this process will affect your free time, relationships, etc. What I want you to do is sit with yourself and mentally and spiritually reflect on whether this is for you.

If, after this reflection, you decide that this is something you were meant to do, and you are ready and willing to make this commitment to yourself, then keep on reading!

There is no set definition of what is involved in an adult B-Mitzvah. Some congregations have programs that are intensive and meant to be completed within six months, while others take an average of two years to complete. If you are unable to find a congregation with the more "streamlined" method, don't worry! Even the longest programs have very flexible schedules and are designed around the busy adult lifestyle. Most programs are offered at night or on weekends and only meet a few times a month for a short period of time during each semester. Some religious schools will also require you to take an "Introduction to Judaism" course along with other Judaic study courses meant to further immerse you in the customs and values of Jewish life. Be sure to check with your synagogue's adult education department for any requirements, books, and fees.

Ready to embark on your journey to passionately read from the Torah? Here are some "pre-B-Mitzvah" preparation steps that you can take to make sure that you are ready to sign up and dive in!

Meeting with Your Rabbi

You don't have to pick up your textbooks or write a check for tuition just yet. Once you've found a congregation that works for you, it would be a good idea to attend a service or two (or 20!), and then meet with the head rabbi, or head of educational programs, to discuss your intentions. At this time, they will ask a series of questions that are intended to make sure you understand exactly what it means to become a B-Mitzvah, and to assess whether they think you are ready to embark on this journey. They will also be able to address any concerns you might have, and answer any questions you have on the program. Ultimately, once you have completed your first meeting, you will be told how to sign up, and who to speak with at the Temple office in order to enroll in the program.

Discuss Your Journey with Family and Friends

When you are a child, it is only natural that the journey to the Torah is just "the way things are," so there are no questions about why, when or how to get started with this program, and how it will affect you and your family. But when you begin this journey as an adult, it's a little different.

For many of you, your decision to become a B-Mitzvah will be greeted with pride and smiles by members of your family and friends. However, if you are taking on this journey at a much later stage in your life—your mid-life, your retirement, your grandparenthood, etc.—or if you are a convert with no friends or family to look to for understanding and support, this is a good time to sit down with people closest in your life and talk to them about what you are doing—and most importantly, what they can expect while you are going through this process. Don't worry—this won't affect your daily routine nearly as much as you think. I can tell you that embarking on this journey is no different than going back to school later in life to obtain your dream degree. I found it very easy to accommodate my schedule for weekly classes, homework, and

Hebrew study.

What you might face is a lack of understanding from gentiles (non-Jews), or your kids or grandkids, who might find it silly that you, as an adult, are going to become B-Mitzvah. Now is the time to tell them why you have chosen to do this, what it means to you, and how important it is that they are there on your special day, and how you would appreciate their support along the way. You should also prepare yourself for the inevitable questioning that will likely arise from doubters in your life, including your own inner voice. This is totally normal, but do not let it discourage you from your mission to get yourself to that scroll!

This is why it is very important to be your own support system and have an open dialogue with your rabbi during this process. It may get very lonely, as people may try to dissuade you from your decision or trivialize its importance to you. You mustn't let them! Keep persevering and know that they will eventually come to understand your decision. And if they don't, at the end of the day, this is your moment, not theirs. Keep moving forward and imagine the look of pride on their faces as you approach the bimah and chant Hebrew from the ancient scroll. I promise you that it will all be worth it!

Putting it All Together: Synagogues in Your Area

Feeling pumped about starting your journey but don't know where to start? There are plenty of resources available to make it easier to determine the synagogue and program that is a good fit for you. Here are a few websites to help you choose the institution that is right for you:

- Reform Judaism: reformjudaism.org
- United Synagogue of Conservative Judaism: uscj.org
- Union of Reform Judaism: urj.org

Shalom, Shalom, Shalom!

The most important thing to remember is that this process is a unique opportunity in your life. It is something that only happens once, and you should enjoy every minute of your journey to the Torah. A fundamental practice in our faith is that of *Shalom*. As you embark on this exciting journey, it is important to take some time for yourself to relax and reflect on how far you have come. It's too easy to live day to day with stress and anxiety; starting something new can only add to the pile. Make it a point to meditate regularly, whether it's daily, weekly, or monthly, and reflect on your reasons for completing this process. Life's stressors can often weigh us down and make studying a great challenge. However, if you continue to focus on your goals, there is no one who can keep you from succeeding. By taking time for yourself and consistently affirming your purpose, you will become unstoppable.

Taking the Next Step

If I've successfully gotten your attention so far without you shutting the book, that means you are ready to make a commitment to your faith and to yourself. You are ready to take the plunge into this whole adult B-Mitzvah thing. Mazel Tov!

If you have yet to choose a congregation to join, now would be a great time to close in on a synagogue where you feel comfortable. You don't necessarily have to join this congregation right away; many congregations will allow you to do your adult B-Mitzvah even if you are not a full member. Keep in mind, however, that prices for these classes and for the program might be a bit higher than what a congregant would normally pay. If you are unable to afford the cost to become a congregant, don't be afraid to have a conversation with the rabbi. Most of the time, and in certain financial situations, the temple will be willing to assist you in whatever way they can to help make paying for this a bit easier. This is an important life event for you, and an important event for the congregation itself. It's not out to make you poor or have you take out a second mortgage on your home. Many people have low or fixed incomes and the rabbi can help. They won't bite—I promise!

After you have chosen your temple, it's time to talk to your temple office, pay the necessary fees, and get your books. Easy!

Depending on the temple, there should be a physical copy of the educational programs schedule in the office; if not, ask about an online version. As mentioned earlier in the chapter, most classes have curricula that are geared toward working adults, and you will find that classes are either in the morning on a weekend, or in the evening on a weekday.

That's enough of the boring stuff. Let's get to why you picked up this book. Let's check out some Hebrew!

Hebrew: "Lots of Dots"

When I first started the program, the thought of learning a new language was both exciting and terrifying. When I was a kid in school I could barely remember how to say "I need to go to the bathroom" in Spanish class. How the heck was I going to pick up a language that was thousands of years old? Every Shabbat service, I would pick up my siddur, gaze at the letters on the page, and wonder how to pronounce them. Feeling defeated, I would turn my head to the transliterations and chant the beautiful songs and prayers with the rest of the congregation. To some that would be enough, but it wasn't enough for me; I had to know more.

On my first day of class, the rabbi and cantor introduced themselves to the class. Fortunately, my class was just me and another woman, who I can easily say was not only a supportive presence through this process, but also someone I can call a close friend. Not all classes are that small; the popularity varies from temple to temple. However, no matter how big or small your class is, at the end of the road you will have a bond with your classmates that can last a lifetime.

This is where a lot of fear comes from when deciding whether or not to sign up for the program. Learning a new language is never easy and takes time, energy, and commitment. When I first considered pursuing my Bat Mitzvah, I could only think of my high school days. I remember loving classes like P.E., art, and music, but my foreign language course was my least favorite class of the week. In college was when I came out of my shell and began to appreciate the eclecticism of subjects that I had at my fingertips. In fact, I took Introduction to Judaism (a requirement of conversion) as part of my undergrad credit in Humanities, while pursing my bachelor's degree. Talk about killing two birds with one stone!

Some of us have been primarily English speakers all our lives;

because of this, learning a new language can be intimidating.

We know what the Hebrew aleph bet looks like and have famil-iarized ourselves with the transliterations of every prayer during Friday night services. Rather than be fearful about learning a new language, let me put a new positive spin on why you should try it. Think of yourself sitting in your synagogue with your siddur in hand. Many of us already attend services weekly and by now have gotten into the habit of flipping to the right page before the rabbi tells us which one to turn to. Now imagine this: you know the prayer transliterations and have committed most of them to muscle memory. Now think of how incredible it would be to chant these prayers by reading them in the original Hebrew. This simple act is so meaningful that it is precisely what motivated me to sit down and write this book. I wanted to encourage people like me to go for it, and to know it's not as scary as it seems. No matter how busy your schedule is, you can do it. I promise you can.

I recall my first day of the program. We received our books and a brief tutorial on the mechanics of reading Hebrew. The cantor told me what I am telling you now: learning Hebrew is actual-ly easier than learning English. The aleph bet, as it is commonly known, consists of reading the letters and vowels as they are; there are fewer letters than in the English alphabet, and there are "lots of dots." To understand this last part, remember the times you've seen Hebrew written out. You may recall seeing dots and dashes above, below, and sometimes to the sides of the letters. These are the vowels. As long as you have a good understanding of them, you can read any Hebrew laid in front of you.

Reading is one thing; understanding is another. But don't fret! Once you understand the foundations of Hebrew and pick up a few core words from your textbooks and prayers, you are well on your way. You can easily expand your vocabulary if you are willing to put in the effort. Make sure you pay attention to class each week; the teachers are, naturally, very good at explaining what the words mean, and how they correspond with other words you may already know. Since you likely already know how many songs and prayers go, you will often find yourself thinking, *Wow, I remember that one*, or *I didn't know that is how that word is actually written!* Learning Hebrew can be quite fun, and my hope is that each week you will learn new words with joy. You're learning a new language, and that is something to be excited about!

As I told you before, I will not bore you with the specifics of learning Hebrew. However, I will give you a sneak peek into what it is like in an effort to alleviate any anxiety you may have about learning a new language.

Now, on to some examples of Hebrew. There are two rules of thumb when it comes to this language's flow. First, you read Hebrew right to left. Why? Some argue that ancient engravers, when chiseling stone tablets, would hold the hammer in their stronger hand (which was usually the right) and hold the chisel in the left hand. The more spiritual reason comes from what is known as the Golden Rule of Judaism, where the right represents chesed (kindness) and the left, gevurah (severity). This important rule teaches us that when we face a decision between kindness and severity, we must choose kindness first. The second, more mechanical, rule of thumb for reading Hebrew is that all words follow a basic pattern: consonant, vowel, consonant, vowel... rinse and repeat.

Take, for example, the word *Shalom,* שָׁלוֹם, (Peace, Hello, Goodbye), which has been drilled into every Jew's head from the beginning of time. I like to think of it as the Jewish *Aloha.*

The word Shalom consists of: Shin ("Sh" sounding letter: שׁ), Kamatz ("ah" the T-shaped sounding vowel under the Shin: ָ), Lamed ("L" sounding letter: ל), Cholam ("oh" sounding vowel, or that little dot on top of the Vav: וֹ), and final Mem ("M" sounding letter: ם). Look at how the word appears and it's quite simple to read. You have (reading from right to left) the consonant, the vowel, the consonant, the vowel...and so on. There are (almost) no tricks in Hebrew. What you see is what you get. Another example is the word Pesach (Passover) —פֶּסַח . Let's break it down — Pei ("P" sounding letter: פ), Segol ("e" sounding vowel: ֶ , those three dots found under Pei), Samekh ("S" sounding letter: ס), Patach (another "ah" sounding vowel that looks like a dash (-) under the Samekh: -), and Chet (glottal "ha" sounding letter: ח).

Getting easier? Just follow the word, from right to left, across the line, look up or down for the vowel—and you've got yourself a word!

Now, when I say there are very few tricks in Hebrew, I mean that with 100% sincerity. Some even say Hebrew is easier than English; I happen to agree.

Take, for example, the word Kol (All): כָּל. In this instance the Kamatz (remember, the T-shaped thingy) is actually a Kamatz Katan and is pronounced "oh" rather than "ah." You will be able to (sometimes not easily) identify that this is the Kamatz Katan as it is usually shown in bold in most *siddurim* (prayer books). That is, unfortunately, the only hint the Hebrew writers give you. It's not written in bold in the Torah (there are *no* vowels in the Torah). It is hard to explain the reason for this exception, but you will get used to reading it this way. Even with Hebrew as simple as it is, you may sometimes pronounce a word incorrectly. Fortunately, your rabbi knows when a Kamatz is actually a Kamatz Katan and will be able to help you to identify it when it changes. Your rabbi and cantor are both your advocates and cheerleaders throughout this process; they want you to look good as possible and succeed at your chanting.

The Not-So-Terrifying Trope

Trope is a unique and interesting mechanism in learning to chant from the Torah. For those more musically inclined, learning trope might come more easily than to someone like me, with no musical ability.

As I've said, this is not a textbook and I do not want to bore you with the specifics of trope. However, you may have heard horror stories of the difficulty of learning trope and chanting. I am here to show you how easy it is to chant from the Torah.

If your class is anything like mine, you won't spend much time with the cantor on learning trope patterns. This concept will be presented to you during the last few months of your coursework. However, you may wonder: what is trope exactly and how does it apply to your studies?

Each verse in the Torah has a specific trope pattern associated with it. You have probably seen these trope patterns as you chanted prayers during Shabbat services; they're often in your siddur. You may not have noticed them, or thought they were part of the Hebrew. Once you are familiar with the common trope melodies, chanting becomes a lot easier. Take, for example, the first part of the V'ahavta. This example has the Hebrew with vowels, but without the trope marks yet:

וְאָהַבְתָּ אֵת יְיָ אֱלֹהֶיךָ, בְּכָל-לְבָבְךָ וּבְכָל-נַפְשְׁךָ וּבְכָל-מְאֹדֶךָ. וְהָיוּ הַדְּבָרִים הָאֵלֶּה אֲשֶׁר אָנֹכִי מְצַוְּךָ הַיּוֹם עַל-לְבָבֶךָ: וְשִׁנַּנְתָּם לְבָנֶיךָ וְדִבַּרְתָּ בָּם בְּשִׁבְתְּךָ בְּבֵיתֶךָ וּבְלֶכְתְּךָ בַדֶּרֶךְ וּבְשָׁכְבְּךָ וּבְקוּמֶךָ. וּקְשַׁרְתָּם לְאוֹת עַל-יָדֶךָ וְהָיוּ לְטֹטָפֹת בֵּין עֵינֶיךָ, וּכְתַבְתָּם עַל מְזֻזוֹת בֵּיתֶךָ וּבִשְׁעָרֶיךָ.

V'ahavta et Adonai Elohecha, b'chol l'vavcha uv'chol nafsh'cha uv'chol m'odecha. V'hayu had'varim ha-eileh asher anochi m'tzav'cha hayom all'vavecha. V'shinantam l'vanecha v'dibarta bam b'shivt'cha b'veitecha uv'lecht'cha vaderech uv'shochb'cha uv'kumecha. Uk'shartam l'ot al yadecha v'hayu l'totafot bein einecha. Uch'tavtam al m'zuzot beitecha uvish'arecha.

Look at the first sentence and sing it once to yourself:

וְאָהַבְתָּ אֵת יְיָ אֱלֹהֶיךָ, בְּכָל-לְבָבְךָ וּבְכָל-נַפְשְׁךָ וּבְכָל-מְאֹדֶךָ.

Look at the first word *V'ahavta* with trope included – וְאָהַבְתָּ

You will see the following trope symbols: Munach (ֻ) and Katon (:).

The V'ahavta contains a very common set of trope that you are likely to recognize as you get familiar with chanting your Torah portion.

The above Munach and Katon each have a specific melody that show how each word is chanted. Trope symbols can sometimes look like a Hebrew vowel; thus, knowing them and their placements will help you in your studies. Take, for example, the Katon (:), whose full name is Zakef Katon. This looks very similar to the Hebrew vowel Sh'va – וֹ. The Sh'va is displayed as two dots, one on top of the other, underneath the letter. Its function is to separate a word into syllables and slow down the word's pronunciation. The Katon, however, is a little bit different. It is still two dots, one on top of the other; however, it comes above a letter in a word. It has a melodic sound which is a moderate rise up and down but starting from a high note. With this tiny bit of information, you should now be able to differentiate the Katon from the Sh'va in the first word of the V'ahavta: וְאָהַבְתָּ .

Shown above, the Sh'va is the first two set of dots, starting on the right, located under the Vav. The Katon is just above the Tav and Kamatz at the end of the word. There are several websites that provide video and audio for each trope melody; I have listed some recommended links at the end of the book. Like vowels, trope does not show up in the Torah, and you will be unable to see it the day of your B-Mitzvah. This is why familiarizing yourself with your Torah portion and the melody is key to your success.

Have you ever tried to remember a song lyric, but you were unable to recall a lyric until you sang the melody in your head? This same technique will prove helpful in the unlikely event that you forget how a word is chanted on your big day; your cantor and rabbi will also be standing with you and will help you at any time if you need it.

Trope is one more useful skill for you to learn on your way to becoming a B-Mitzvah. Never turn down any skills that could potentially prove useful in your development. Have an open mind and you can easily have trope work in your favor, even if you think learning it is difficult. Remember when you thought Hebrew was going to be hard? Look at you now! You're practically an expert! All you needed was the courage to proceed. It's no different with trope.

Again, you will study trope melodies with your cantor during your B-Mitzvah classes, but familiarizing yourself early will benefit you in the long run. If you are computer savvy, you can search the internet or YouTube for trope patterns. You will find plenty of videos and lessons from cantors that provide helpful instruction on how these patterns work. It's a good idea to check with your cantor to find out if the trope you find online is the same as what your temple uses; sometimes trope can be slightly different from one temple to the next.

I am not saying that to master one's Torah portion you *have* to become an expert with trope—far from it. I know it seems easier said than done, but look at it this way: have you ever been on a long drive or at your home with the radio on? A new song comes on, and then comes on again every couple of hours as you keep driving or you conduct your daily business. The song might only exist as background noise to you; then one day, you hear the song and are able to hum along to the melody or even sing some of the lyrics. This is what happens when you study and learn trope patterns.

Try to focus more on trope patterns and less on how the trope looks on paper. Relying on what trope symbols look like may help you when practicing, but it won't help you on the day of your B-Mitzvah, as the Torah is written only with Hebrew letters—no vowels, no trope.

Gaining a basic familiarity with trope melodies will help a great deal when you are finally up on the bimah. Even if you forget a word or a phrase, take a minute and focus on what you remember from studying the trope melody. It is amazing how useful muscle memory is when you go over a melody a few hundred times.

It might also be helpful to learn the trope patterns and memorize the melody before the words, like you would memorize a song. Once you get the music (trope) down, and then learn to read the lyrics (Hebrew), you can put the two pieces together with ease.

When I was going through the process, I practiced my parts, prayers, and songs so much that I was able to chant my parashah without even looking at it. I even sang it to myself on the train to work. Even though I committed my six verses to memory, I would occasionally look at the copy of my parashah without vowels or trope and read each word aloud, focusing on each letter. This kept my muscle memory active, so that by the time my Bat Mitzvah day arrived I was very confident in what I was reading.

One thing you may find useful is to ask your cantor to record your Torah portion so you can listen to it at every opportunity. Then, take your Torah portion with trope and go through it line by line; don't move on to the next until you are confident in the first. Each week go over each verse you have learned with your teacher so you know you have it down. Don't be nervous; you will only have a maximum of six to nine verses to read. Learning a few verses each week and committing them to memory will help you to master your "song" within some months' time—or even less time than that.

Practice, practice, practice, and keep going and keep doing. Even dedicating just one extra day each week on top of your B-Mitzvah class will be beneficial to your learning. Some weeks you might be able to commit more time than others, but as long as you make an effort to study and to continue keeping the words and melodies fresh in your mind, you will be good to go.

Now for the part that I was most excited about when I went through the program. Let's learn next how you receive your Torah portion.

Your Torah Portion

Which parashah you will read on the day of your B-Mitzvah will depend on the time of the year on the Jewish calendar. A *parashah* is a section of the Torah. Each week there is a new parashah designated to read from the Torah. While the Jewish calendar follows a lunar cycle, the secular calendar measures the earth's rotation around the sun. Because of this, your Torah portion might be entirely different from someone else's, even if their parashah falls on the same day and the same time on the secular calendar the following year. For example, my portion was Parashah B'har Behukotai from the Book of Leviticus, Chapter 25, verses 19-24. My portion corresponded with the date 23 Iyyar 5777, or May 19, 2017. The next year, however, May 19, 2018 fell on 5 Sivan 5778 with the parashah for that week being Bamidbar. Although the *parashot* (plural) appear to move throughout each secular calendar year, in reality they stay the same on the Jewish calendar. This is the same reason that Hanukkah can sometimes occur in November in one year and then December in another year.

One of the most important things you should do when you select your Torah portion is take the time to understand the parashah for that week. This is especially important because the verses you will be reading are only part of the entire parashah. Not taking the time to read and understand the message behind the entire parashah for that week will make it harder to write your D'var Torah. The next chapter will focus on writing a lovely D'var for your service.

A lot of people skim over the parashah for the week, pick bits and pieces of what they understand, and use those tidbits to write their interpretation. While this may save you some time, I strongly suggest you get a firm grasp on your parashah instead. By reading it closely, you may actually find several verses you identify with.

After our rabbi gave us the assignment of opening our Torah and turning to the parashah for that week, my first thought was, *Oh my gosh this is a lot of reading!* My classmate and I even expressed our concern to our rabbi. She encouraged us to tackle each section little by little and highlight which sections stood out to us. This strategy made everything much easier.

When I began the program, I was working a nine-to-five job, mostly in front of a computer. This made it rather challenging to make time to study after work, as I only had an hour or two a night, with only a few nights off in between. I often found myself feeling tired and overwhelmed, and it took all I had to turn off the TV, open my book, and study. In the end, I'm happy I did.

As an avid reader I tend to read at a fast pace so that I can get to the ending as quickly as possible. Due to this what I would call character flaw, my first tactic in tackling my Torah portion was skimming through each page to seek out the relevant information. You'd think this would get me to where I wanted to be faster, instead of spending what I thought would be countless hours reading every word. Unfortunately, the way I was accustomed to doing things in my work life was not going to work for this project. I'm not saying you have to dedicate 10-hour days to learning your Torah portion; just don't half-ass it. You'll thank me later.

It's easy to feel overwhelmed. Just take a deep breath, turn off distractions for an hour, and focus on what you're reading. A parashah can be long, and the only way to learn it all is to take the time to read it properly. For example, I found that I disagreed with my parashah and was even shocked by what I read; so much so that I felt the need to discuss it with my rabbi.

For instance, in one of my readings I learned of a G-d that was generous and kind to those who followed the laws that were commanded of us. That, I fully agreed with. The next section I read spoke of the many horrible consequences that could occur if you went against what G-d had commanded. I won't get into the detail about what horrors I read in that chapter, but needless to say it was something I was really going to have to wrap my head around if I was going to put a more positive spin on it. I encourage you to talk to your rabbi about anything you disagree with; they are familiar with what you are reading and will be able to provide you with an entirely new perspective on your parashah.

I spoke to our cantor about how I was confused that such a wrathful G-d and such a nurturing G-d could be one and the same. She reminded me that the Torah is not a document that is updated constantly. It had to be thought about in the historical context of the time. It was possible that the Jewish people may have been struggling when that particular passage was written, and considered leaving the faith, worshipping false gods, or straying from what G-d had commanded. The fear of a harsh punishment from G-d if they were to stray likely saved our religion and culture from extinction. This spoke to me on a deeper level, and I began looking for ways to apply what I was reading to issues of today. I was able to correlate much of current events with what I read in my Torah portion for that week.

Remember that you are not expected to be an expert on what you are reading; in fact, for many of you, this will be your first time reading the words of the Torah. You have many people, such as your rabbi, to help you understand what you are reading so you can give your interpretation to the congregation.

There are plenty of relevant events in the world that you can apply to your Torah portion. Keep in mind that what you are reading was written in the hopes of making us the best Jews we can be according to the laws of Judaism. You are not a bad Jew if you don't understand or even disagree with what is written. The best part of being Jewish is being encouraged from a young age to ask as many questions as possible. To this end, I encourage you to ask questions as you continue your B-Mitzvah studies. You don't have to go through this alone—there are plenty of resources out there to help you get a firm grasp on what you are reading. I promise you, if you take the time to master your parashah, you will feel incredibly accomplished on your big day. By taking the time to give it your all and focus on the task at hand, you will find that you only further your connection with G-d and Judaism. Remember, there is a reason you chose to take this extra step in your Jewish education. Hold that reason in your heart during each step of the program.

Hear Ye, Hear Ye!
Writing Your D'var Torah

Personally, this was the most challenging aspect of the process for me. Hebrew, as I've said before, is easy to pick up; the hard part is reading, understanding, and teaching your Torah portion to others. Anyone can pronounce words in another language, but it takes more practice to actually know what those words mean.

The D'var Torah is not something you can hash out during an episode of your favorite show. You will require a few days, if not a month, to understand what you will be teaching people on the day of your B-Mitzvah. Don't worry; your rabbi will be your editor, and will ensure that your D'var is perfect by the time you approach the bimah.

There are some things you should keep in mind as you are writing your D'var. First, remember that everyone interprets Torah portions differently. This is the best thing about the Torah; it can be interpreted in so many ways that there is no right or wrong way to do so. Think about that for a minute: the Torah was written thousands of years ago, and yet you will still find many parashot that relate to events of today or even to something deep inside yourself. You may also find passages that will shock you. In my portion, B'har Behukotai, there are several passages about a quite scary version of G-d. I remember reading this portion and my heart raced as I read each sentence. I thought to myself, *This is not the G-d that I know,* and I brought this up to my rabbi the following week in class. As you discuss your week's parashah with your rabbi, you will find that everything written in the Torah can be explained by what I mentioned earlier. Since the Torah is not a "constant document" (meaning that it cannot be edited for current context), it must be interpreted with the understanding that its "literal meaning" was geared more for people reading it during the time it was written. What do I mean by that? Let's look at my Torah portion, B'har Behukotai, as an example. In this parashah, there is a laundry list of rules that we as Jews are expected to follow, as well as a list of blessings and curses that we will receive if we obey or disobey a particular rule. When I discussed this with the cantor that week, she explained that there may have been a period of unrest among the Jewish people at the time this was written; a time when people were considering worshipping false idols and turning away from their Jewish roots. This is the most likely reason the Behukotai chapter was written. You could say that the "G-d fearing" chapters were just that: meant to scare people with the consequences they could face should they steer away from what G-d commanded of them. As I mentioned before, this is just one interpretation that you could derive from reading this parashah. It was not meant to be taken literally, nor could it possibly be taken literally in modern times. That is why getting a firm grasp on what your parashah is about is so important.

Trust me when I say this sounds scarier than it actually is. This is one of the best moments of the whole process; you have the opportunity to take center stage and get creative in explaining the week's lesson and how it applies to current events.

As you do research to write your draft, you'll discover that much of what is in the Torah can still apply today. You might have to put your own spin on it to get your point across, but remember: there are no wrong answers here, and your rabbi will be there 100% of the way to ensure what you are writing makes sense and is the best it can be by the time your B-Mitzvah comes. This isn't a textbook, and I won't waste your time explaining the mechanics of writing your D'var Torah. That will be explained to you during your coursework.

You'll be amazed what you can develop with a little time and commitment. You've mastered the language, and you're not too far from approaching the bimah, depending on when you're reading this. If you've made it this far, then writing your D'var Torah will be easy-peasy.

To help you understand what sort of thing you're going to write, I'll end this section with my personal D'var; not only to show you what it looks like, but also to prove that if a 29-year-old, full-time insurance broker, with a husband, bills, and a very active and busy day-to-day can accomplish the task of writing a D'var, then you can, too! Believe me—it can be done.

My D'var Torah: Behar-Behukotai

By Christine Machlin

As Susan shared, we have chanted from B'har of the combined Torah portions B'har Bechukotai. In Behar, we learn about the Sabbatical Year, or the Jubilee year, where we are told to let the land in which we grow crops rest for one year, and to forgive any debts that have been owed to us in the past seven years. In Behukotai, there are even more rules still. We hear of the blessings we receive for following and obeying the laws that G-d has given us, as well as the even greater number of curses that could arise should we go against what G-d has commanded us to do.

In our Torah, we receive so many rules and commandments. For some Jews, observing all commandments, praying three times a day, and studying our texts makes for a "good Jew." For others, feeling like we are good Jews may mean to keep Shabbat every week, whether it be to light the candles at home or with our fellow congregants at Friday night service. Give tzedakah, fast on Yom Kippur, become Bar or Bat Mitzvah, participate in Sederim at Passover, and shake the grogger on Purim. Meaning, it is our job to keep the Jewish calendar observances.

For me, it appears that structured observance and temple obligations make it easier to be a "good" Jew. In this aspect, when we are in a religious setting like a temple, church, or mosque, it is quite easy to be a "holy person," because we know the steps and how to behave and act at our religious institutions.

But I ask you, how many of us really LIVE the commandments, and live a Jewish life outside of the synagogue? That is actually much harder. When we are not in temple, when there is no rabbi present, it gets very easy to press the pause button on our other religious obligations on how to behave as Jews outside of the temple.

We are taught that being a Jew is acting with kindness and compassion, asking questions, being grateful to G-d for all the gifts we are given every day, to help those in need, and to keep the Sabbath. A day of rest should perhaps be the simplest and least challenging to observe. After working a hard week, to sit back and relax, no work, no cooking, no requirement to labor; how it could be made any easier on us as human beings? I can stay home, relax, breathe and rejuvenate. Except, there are often competing activities for our attention like social opportunities and more.

When it comes to the other Jewish values outside of temple, they can be more challenging. There are times even in my own life where I ask myself, how many times this week did I express gratitude for what I have received? How many times did I give tzedakah outside of my Shabbat obligations? There is so much more to being a Jew than the synagogue.

Judaism calls us to observe our values in a variety of sacred ways outside of calendar and ritual observance. Ethical matters, such as letting debts go free as mentioned in our portion of B'har. In the Jubilee year, people who owed debts were slaves to whom they were obligated. Land that was taken belonged to those whom it was owed for seven years, and on the Jubilee year, it was returned to its original owner. Slaves who were slaves as a debt were allowed to return to their families, and their debts, no matter what, were considered repaid.

We learn patience and forgiveness from this is. How many times have we gotten in fights with friends and family over money, pride, or personal gains that have resulted in us not speaking to each other for years and for some, the rest of our lives? How good did it feel to be in the quarrel with that person, and how great did it feel at the time when we talked it through and made amends? We, as a society, are losing our ability to forgive. Often times it's our own stubbornness and the inability let things go that prevents us from living full happy lives without anger and resentment.

We live every day in monotonous steps that get us from Monday to Friday, living most of our lives through autopilot. If we could just learn to slow down and turn off our autopilot, even if just for a few minutes a day, we would allow ourselves to take a minute and truly appreciate the world around us, the people in our lives, and all the little miracles we are given every day.

The great Ferris Bueller said it best: "Life moves pretty fast, if you don't stop and look around once in a while, you could miss it." Let go of the stress, let go of the anger, turn off the autopilot, and replace it with happiness, compassion, and gratitude. A little tweak in our everyday routine is all we need to really reap the benefits of all the miracles and gifts we are given every day.

Shabbat Shalom.

Writing Your Jewish Journey Speech

This is probably the most powerful project that you will be tasked to write for your B-Mitzvah. It involves some major soul searching to dig down to the root of why you are doing what you are doing, and what led you to where you are today. Your Jewish journey tells your story to the congregation and is a moment for you to tell your truth. This is a time to tell those you hold dear something they may not know about you. Perhaps family or friends have always questioned your religious life choices, and at this time you can affirm what makes you YOU and why you chose to never change. This could also be a moment to express gratitude to those in your life who have stuck by you and have supported you in life, and during your journey to becoming a B-Mitzvah. Depending on how many people are in your class, either your whole class will step up to tell their individual stories or the rabbi will select one student to be the representative for the class as a whole. If you aren't selected, it's not because the rabbi disliked what you had written; it's likely because of what they feel will most closely match the tone of the service. Regardless of whether you're selected, I would advise you to take this project seriously. Not only does it give your classmates and rabbi an opportunity to learn more about you and the path you have walked, but it also gives you the opportunity to identify who you are from a Judaic perspective.

When I first started writing my speeches, I found it very hard to get what I wanted to say out onto the page. I couldn't get out of my own way and overthought every word I wrote. I put too much pressure on myself and deleted line after line of what, in hindsight, were well written and powerful statements. In frustration, I took a few days off to reflect on the person I was and what I wanted to write about. It's amazing what you can come up with when you escape your own mind for a bit and really think about yourself as a

Jew. You have spent a significant amount of time as a Jew, but have you ever sat down to reflect on the kind of Jewish person you are? Rather than sit in front of your computer and write your speech, get out of the house. Take a walk, go to the gym, and spend time with family, friends, or at a park by yourself. Think about everything that has brought you to here and now, to this day of the week, this chapter of the book, and ask yourself, *Why have I chosen to be a B-Mitzvah?*

When you have the answer to that question, you are ready to write your speech. Let the words flow out of your fingers and mind and onto the keyboard. Keep going until there's nothing left for you to say. It doesn't matter if it's a hot load of steaming garbage; once you have every little detail you want down on the page, you can think about editing. The rabbi will probably give you a page limit, which will likely be three pages or less. Take what you have written and really read everything you had to say. You will find that most of what you've written isn't garbage, and is in fact inspiring. After reading the last sentence, you should have a better idea of what you should say, and after a few more rounds of reviewing and editing, you will have your masterpiece.

After your speech is perfected, reread your work. Keep your speech with you even after your B-Mitzvah, and let it remind you where you have come from, the person you are at this moment in your life, and the person you want to become. Remember, this will more than likely be a treasured keepsake for your kids, grandkids, and generations after you.

And, once again to provide some guidance, the next page is my Jewish Journey speech to aid as another example of what you could write.

My Jewish Journey

By Christine Machlin

In my young adult life, I've been and have become many things. A daughter, a student, a graduate, a girlfriend, and recently...a wife. I've also endured challenges, faced hardships, and rejoiced in many accomplishments... the most important of which being when I became a Jew.

It's been nearly six years, and although I can speak of this now with joy and pride, I will tell you that my journey was not easy.

I was raised Roman Catholic by an extremely loving and observant family. I attended private school at both a Catholic elementary school and high school. It was not until my first year of college that I got to experience wearing "regular clothes" to school rather than a uniform. My first week of my freshman year, I think I wore the same outfit more than twice... on a "starving college student" budget, a new wardrobe was not on the agenda.

What WAS on the agenda was my desire to transition from a naive adolescent to an educated, responsible, mature adult. I took this as my opportunity to figure out who I really was, and if I was dissatisfied with the result, I now had the opportunity to focus on who I wanted to become.

After five years and three changes in my major, I was approaching my college graduation, and yet at the same time another transition in my life was quickly approaching. Early on in my college endeavors I faced the tough reality of questioning my faith, and that too was something I had to do some major reflecting on to decide on the religious person I wanted to become...that is what brought me to Judaism.

I give major credit to both my Catholic upbringing and to my parents in providing me with the foundations, values, and the knowledge of what it means to truly believe in the power of faith, and guiding me in my relationship with G-d.

My journey in becoming a Jew was a momentous time in my young adult life. Everything was called into question, and my relationship with my faith, with my family, and especially with my parents, was turned upside down. There were moments where I wanted to give up, where I felt lost, and where I truly questioned whether this was something that perhaps I had made the wrong decision in pursing. I cannot thank Rabbi Michael and his wife Caryn (both here today) enough for being there for me during this uphill journey I was pursuing, for providing me with comfort and encouragement that I truly needed, and for welcoming me in to their home for Jewish holidays when I had nowhere else to celebrate.

Like many difficult moments in everyone's life, the dark moment passed, I met with the Beit Din, I entered the mikvah one person, and walked out a Jew...reborn, spiritually fulfilled, and finally complete...and I've never looked back.

My life has brought to me so many simchas, from my conversion, to marrying the love of my life...and today life has given me one more...today I am a Bat Mitzvah.

In the past two years, I have learned so much, and have an even greater understanding of my Jewish identity. I've especially learned a few important things: 1 — that Hebrew is not as hard as it looks (no, really!), and 2 — that no matter how far you are in life, you are never done learning.

I am truly grateful to have been given this opportunity to continue my education, and develop even stronger roots in my Jewish identity.

I'd like to thank Rabbi Sarah, and Cantors Jen and Shana for guiding me through these past two years. You have all been a tremendous inspiration to me, and I cannot thank you enough for giving me the motivation and strong desire to keep moving forward in my faith...the road will not stop here.

To my incredible husband who continues to encourage and support me in my journey, who shares with me the importance of our faith and traditions, as well as the importance of living a Jewish life and passing those values to our future family. To my family who have known me my entire life, and to my family who have recently welcomed me in to their lives...words cannot express how much you being here has meant to me. I thank each and every one of you for the vital role you each have played in my life. Your continued support and love I truly treasure and I thank you from the bottom of my heart for being here to celebrate with me today... To my parents...I know my journey to get here was not an easy one for you... but your love and acceptance over the past few years, and your support in being here to celebrate with me today means so much more to me than you can possibly imagine, and I love you so very much for that. To Rabbi Michael and his wife Caryn for getting me to this point, for being incredible mentors to me, officiating on the day I married my Bashert, and for your suggestion to come to Temple Beth Hillel as our family synagogue. I appreciate everything you have done for me, and for continuing to be a valued part of our lives. And lastly, a big thank you to my mother- and father-in-law not only for this beautiful tallit, but also for accepting me into your family as your new daughter, sharing your home with me each holiday and Shabbat, and especially to my mother-in-law Helen, for teaching me the secret of making the most exceptional matzo ball soup known to man...and that secret I'm taking to the grave.

Baruch atah Adonai, Eloheinu Melech haolam, shehecheyanu, v'kiy'manu, v'higianu laz'man hazeh. Praise to You, G-d, Sovereign of the Universe for giving us life, sustaining us, and enabling us to reach this season.

Prepping for the Bimah

The weeks leading up to your B-Mitzvah are both exciting and stressful. At this time, you are finished with the big picture and focusing on the smaller details, such as accommodations for family coming from out of town, details for the oneg, and obtaining ritual items needed for your B-Mitzvah ceremony. The first is a tallit, or prayer shawl, made of cotton or wool. Tallitot (plural) come in a variety of styles and are designed for both men and women. There are different styles of tallitot depending on which movement of Judaism you identify with. We will dive more into the significance of the tzitzit and the proper way to put on your tallit in the chapters ahead.

Another item to start shopping for is a kippah, or yarmulke, the traditional head covering. Kippot (plural) can be customized in a variety of ways, with a plethora of design and fabric options. There are plenty of vendors you can research that offer a variety of styles for you to choose from. There are also a variety of companies that will design a kippah with a matching tallit based on your exact specifications. The following are some examples of kippot for both males and females:

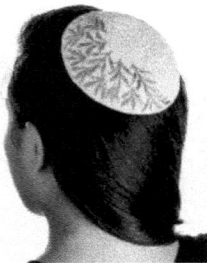

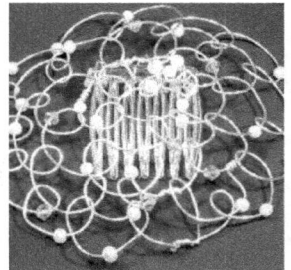

The last item you should consider is a yad—the pointer used when reading from the Torah. As with the other previously mentioned ritual items, there are also a variety of yadayim (plural) to choose from on the market. Again, a quick internet search or visit to your local Judaica store will provide you with a good variety of options to choose from.

Now the yad isn't necessarily a requirement for the big day, but some people think of it as memento that they will pass down to either their children or grandchildren. Don't worry if you don't have a yad; the Torah at your congregation comes fully equipped with one that you are more than welcome to use, which is common practice. Here is an example of a yad for reference:

It's easy to become overwhelmed in the last-minute details, but don't sweat the small stuff. Stay focused on why you're doing what you're doing. Much like the days before a wedding, little details can become your priority. But also like your wedding, the only thing that matters at this time is the huge step you are taking in an important ritual. The B-Mitzvah is a rite of passage in a Jew's life, and not something that should be taken lightly.

The B-Mitzvah ritual as we understand it has existed for hundreds of years. Think about how special you are that you will soon be among the millions of Jews who have been called to the Torah to read from its ancient text. There are more than 3,700 synagogues in the United States alone. If only one person per synagogue were called to the Torah each week, we'd be up to almost 200,000 readers in a year. Many of our ancestors endured suffering and death to protect our Torah and to ensure that this tradition continues throughout the generations.

It will soon be your responsibility to teach the words of the Torah to your congregation and join the long line of people who have taken this journey. It is your responsibility to ensure that this tradition never stops, and that your children and your children's children join the line along with you.

Your journey does not stop at the Torah. For centuries, our faith, rituals, culture, and people have fought to exist. The memory of their struggle and everything our ancestors have done to make sure we continue as a people should never be forgotten. Thus, it's important that you continue to keep our customs alive and thriving. We will touch more on what you can do to keep the Jewish faith alive in your own life and in the world around you in the coming chapters.

During your B-Mitzvah, you will be required to lead a service. The difficulty of this task will depend on how familiar you are with a Friday or Saturday Shabbat service. Whether you are a regular at Shabbat services or only go during the High Holy Days will not matter; all you need is a basic understanding of the rituals performed, most of which you may have probably already experienced. You won't need to be an expert, but you certainly want to study, be familiar with your temple's siddur (prayer book), and have a basic understanding of each prayer. A lot of this you will cover in your B-Mitzvah classes. As I said before, your rabbi will not leave you hanging on this day. It is their job to help you shine, and if you follow their advice and listen to everything they teach you, you will be just fine.

During your rehearsals leading up to the big day, you will work with the rabbis and cantors on each part of the service: your parts, your classmate's parts, when to sit, when to stand, etc. Feel free to ask as many questions as you need to so that you are very comfortable with all elements in the service. Don't worry if you still have some questions after your rehearsal; your rabbi can answer any questions or concerns you have.

The time leading up to the service may give you butterflies in your stomach, but remember: this is one of the greatest moments of your adult life. You've studied hard and you've paid your dues. You might not know everything, but that's okay. I promise you, no matter what happens that day, it will be the best day ever.

After classes concluded for me and my B-Mitzvah partner, Susan, there were still a few weeks to go before the actual service. This may be the case for you. It's important to keep all the Hebrew, trope, and prayers fresh in your mind in the time between when your classes end and when your service is. For some of you, going regularly to Shabbat services will be enough to keep everything fresh. However, for those whose schedules make it difficult to attend services regularly, you might have to get creative in making time in your schedule to study independently. You may find it helpful to arrange to meet with your classmates for coffee or dinner and bring your books. Go through the elements of the service, practice your speeches, chant your Torah portion, and help those who are struggling. My partner and I studied many times on our own before our service. We met both in person and online. Whether you meet in person or teleconference is your choice, but you should keep practicing to keep all the knowledge fresh in your mind. The best thing you can do for yourself is to give yourself a break and accept that what will be, will be. Even if you mess up, jumble a word, or your mind goes blank during your parashah, you shouldn't worry. No one will notice, and if they do, they will not care if you make a mistake. Everyone who will be there knows how hard it is to stand up in front of a large group of people; they understand how scary this can be and how hard you have worked to get to this moment. No one is going to laugh at you if you make a mistake;

even if you do, I guarantee that about 90% of the people there will not notice. We are our own worst critics; this is our nature as humans. Just breathe, relax, practice, practice, practice, focus, do your absolute best and you will be successful. If nothing else, remember the importance of this moment. It is your day, your 15 minutes of fame, and no matter what, it will be spectacular.

Now, you've learned everything there is to know to become a B-Mitzvah...it's now the time for the big moment. It's time for the big day!

The Big Day

I can't begin to tell you what an incredible day this was for me. It was the day I had spent two years studying for. I remember when I first started my classes I looked down at my Hebrew book at those strange characters on the page, and I thought to myself, *How the heck am I going to read all of this?* It was a nerve-wracking time, but there was nothing like the feeling of going through all that study, all that hard work, and all those nights staying up late to make sure that I was prepared for class the next morning, only to wake up on the morning of my Bat Mitzvah knowing that after today, my life would never be the same. There were a lot of emotions pulsating through me one after the other. I felt fear, joy, and a bit of sadness knowing that my Sunday mornings would no longer consist of class at 8:00 a.m. followed by a few hours of study at home. No, today I was done. At the beginning, two years felt like an eternity. But on the day of my Bat Mitzvah, it felt like I blinked, and I was done.

As I mentioned in the last chapter, in the weeks leading up to the big day I was overwhelmed by worry and trying to make everything perfect for this day. But when the day finally came, I was surprised to feel an overwhelming sense of calm and peace, as though a weight had been lifted. That day, I felt closer with G-d than I think I ever had in my entire life. As my heart raced, I felt excitement with visions running through my head of my husband, parents, in-laws, and family as I looked out from the bimah after I completed my Torah portion. I pictured the looks of pride on their faces at my future accomplishment. I imagined my future children going through this process years from now. When I signed up for this class, I guess I didn't realize how powerful this time in my life was until the very day arrived.

A lot of us are encouraged by our parents at a young age to become B-Mitzvah—so much so that it becomes more of a routine to children than something of a significant value. However, as an adult, it is so much different. You chose to do this. No one forced this on you, and no one held you accountable but yourself. There are a lot of people out there who never chose this for themselves and decided that this was not the path they were going to take, and that's okay. But you did, and you should feel so proud of yourself for taking this incredible journey.

Today can be full of overwhelming thoughts and feelings that can easily get the best of you. This is why you should take some time off before your service and take some time for yourself. You may choose to spend time with your family—have them take you out to breakfast, go to a movie, get a massage, get your nails and hair done. Anything you can do to spoil yourself today is greatly encouraged and will help calm any last-minute nerves you might have. It doesn't seem like something you need right now when you are reading this and are possibly at the beginning your journey; but trust me, you'll thank me for this advice when your moment finally comes.

If you so choose, you can also go to the mikvah (ritual bath) on this day, as a lot of people do on important simchas in their lives. The mikvah is a beautiful experience. Below is a photo of me at a mikvah at the American Jewish University in Los Angeles, California.

People choose to enter the mikvah just before their B-Mitzvah as a means of signifying the transition from their life before their B-Mitzvah to the new journey and path they will walk as a Son or Daughter of the Commandment (B-Mitzvah). Whether you choose to do this or not is entirely up to you and can only add to your experience. Do not worry if you do not choose to do this; it is not normally a requirement of completing the program.

If you are interested in submerging in the mikvah or would like more information on what a mikvah is and where you can find one in your area, please see the resources section at the end of the book.

As you can now imagine, the possibilities of what you can do to make time for yourself on the day or night before your B-Mitzvah are endless. As long as you enter your synagogue with a clear heart, a relaxed state of mind, and a genuine feeling of readiness to proceed, then you have done everything right.

It's finally the moment you've been waiting for. There is no official answer to what exactly one can expect on their special day, as everyone's journey and service is different both emotionally and spiritually. At this point, you most likely have rehearsed with your rabbi, who will have walked you through everything that will be happening today, as well as provided you with parts that you personally will play in the service. During rehearsal, you will also have had the opportunity to read your portion directly from the Torah and get a feel of what it will be like when you are actually up there. You're ready!

The service will begin as any other Shabbat service. The second part of the service will consist of the B-Mitzvah. How long your service will take depends on how many people are in your class. For example, my class only had two people, which made our service only a little longer than a normal Friday night Shabbat service. When inviting guests to your service, it is probably best to ask your rabbi about how long you should advise your guests to set aside for your big day. For you, the length of your service will not matter, because it will be over before you know it and it will seem like no time has passed at all.

Therefore, it is important to be 100% present today and take in every single moment. Soak up every emotion and detail during your service. Focus and feel the joy and happiness in your heart during each moment. Granted, some worry and nerves are completely normal since you have never led a service before. However, try not to let nerves and fear get the best of you today. Keep telling yourself that you are ready, this is your moment, and that with faith you can accomplish anything. Today only proves what you have accomplished. It's a big deal—enjoy it!

The first important part of the B-Mitzvah ceremony is when your rabbi presents you with your tallit, or prayer shawl, that we as Jews wear to remind us of the commandments of the Torah, which are represented by the *tzitzit*, the specially tied fringes on the corners of the tallit.

Your rabbi will have your tallit ready to go for you for just this moment. You will be invited to hold your tallit in front of you, and then the following prayer is recited:

בָּרוּךְ אַתָּה יְיָ אֱלֹהֵינוּ מֶלֶךְ הָעוֹלָם אֲשֶׁר קִדְּשָׁנוּ בְּמִצְוֹתָיו, וְצִוָּנוּ לְהִתְעַטֵּף בַּצִּיצָת.

Baruch ata Adonai, Eloheinu, Melech ha'olam asher kidishanu b'mitz'votav v'tzivanu l'hit'ateif ba-tzitzit.

Once this prayer is said, you will kiss both ends of your tallit and hug it around you.

In the next part of the service, you and your classmates will all be invited up to the bimah by your rabbi and presented with the Torah. Again, depending on how many people in your group, you will be handed a Torah and will either hold on to one, or pass it down in the line of your classmates to the last person. The rabbi and cantor will then present you to the congregation, say a few kind words, and will conclude with you and your classmates walking the Torah around the synagogue. People will touch their prayer books to the Torah and shout words of congratulation, such as *Mazel tov!* This may provide a bit of emotional relief from any nerves you have. Greeting the congregation and having them shout words of encouragement will fill your heart and is guaranteed to get you in a happy mindset for when you read from the scroll. The Torah you all will be reading from will then be opened and presented; any other Torahs will be placed back in the ark.

Each student, along with close family, will then be called up for an *aliyah*—the blessing before and after reading the Torah. If you were raised Jewish, have been a regular at temple services, or have a slight familiarity with temple prayers, this one will probably be familiar to you. The blessing goes like this:

Before reading the Torah, you say:

בָּרְכוּ אֶת יְיָ הַמְבֹרָךְ

Barchu et Adonai hamvorach.

The congregation says:

בָּרוּךְ יְיָ הַמְבֹרָךְ לְעוֹלָם וָעֶד

Baruch Adonai ham-vo-rach l'olam va-ed.

You respond:

בָּרוּךְ יְיָ הַמְבֹרָךְ לְעוֹלָם וָעֶד.
בָּרוּךְ אַתָּה יְיָ אֱלֹהֵינוּ מֶלֶךְ הָעוֹלָם, אֲשֶׁר בָּחַר בָּנוּ מִכָּל הָעַמִּים,
וְנָתַן לָנוּ אֶת תּוֹרָתוֹ.
בָּרוּךְ אַתָּה יְיָ, נוֹתֵן הַתּוֹרָה.

Baruch Adonai ham-vo-rach l'olam va-ed. Baruch ata Adonai, Eloheinu Melech ha-olam, asher ba-char-banu mee-kol ha-a-mim, v'na-tan lanu et torato. Baruch ata Adonai, notein haTorah.

Don't worry about memorizing it. The rabbi will have a copy of this blessing, although you want to make sure to be quite familiar with the Hebrew.

Once you complete the first part of the aliyah, it is now your moment to shine. Everything you have been preparing yourself for, all the studying you have done, and the countless hours of learning you have pursued have led you to this moment. It is now time for you to chant your Torah portion to the congregation.

Again, everyone's experience with this particular moment is different, but your experience will mean more to you than almost any event in your adult life. My rabbi said it best when she was prepping us for the big day: "Once you complete your studies and become a Bat Mitzvah you are never the same, in a spectacular way."

Once you have chanted your Torah portion, there is an incredible feeling of being a part of a special group of people who have come before you and have become B-Mitzvah. After all those people who have spoken to you about their journey, and who have encouraged you to become a B-Mitzvah, it is now your turn to keep the tradition going, and this is a responsibility not to be taken lightly. The tradition of the B-Mitzvah has been around for multiple generations and it is important that we not let it die.

The ancient text that you are reading from is the language and story of our people. It is a scroll that many have tried to take away from us. We have fought and died to protect what is contained in the Torah and every time the tradition of the B-Mitzvah is passed down through the generations, we continue to fight for our language and culture to survive. You contribute to this fight by completing this rite of passage. The significance of what you are doing is even more powerful than you can imagine.

Take a deep breath just before you read your portion. There is no rush to begin. Try to center yourself and become immersed in the moment, even if just for a few seconds. When you're ready, grab the yad and begin. As you're reading your portion, home in on the words you are speaking; you might not know what every word you are saying means, but at this point you have read enough of your portion to understand its message. Keep that message in your heart as you chant each word from the Torah.

After you are finished, it is now time to complete your aliyah and read the blessing after the Torah is read, which is:

After reading the Torah, you say:

בָּרוּךְ אַתָּה יְיָ אֱלֹהֵינוּ מֶלֶךְ הָעוֹלָם, אֲשֶׁר נָתַן לָנוּ תּוֹרַת אֱמֶת, וְחַיֵּי עוֹלָם נָטַע בְּתוֹכֵנוּ. בָּרוּךְ אַתָּה יְיָ, נוֹתֵן הַתּוֹרָה.

Baruch ata Adonai, eloheinu melech ha-olam, asher natan lanu torat emet, v'cha-yei olam na-ta b'to-chei-nu. Baruch ata Adonai, notein ha-Torah.

As soon as those last words leave your lips, you are officially a B-Mitzvah! At this moment people will be shouting "Mazel Tov!" Your family will be standing by you, and your rabbi will be hugging you and sending you well wishes and love along with the entire congregation, who will be singing the popular song *Siman Tov U'Mazel Tov*. Feel the love and really take in every bit of this moment, as it is your moment in the spotlight.

A lot of people are not public speakers, and conjuring up the courage to get up on the bimah in front of a bunch of people, read from the Torah, and teach the congregation of the meaning behind the parashah for that week is not an easy task. It can be quite nerve-racking and scary for some, which is why the moment after you have become a B-Mitzvah is very special. Every fearful and nervous feeling that you had in the time leading up to the Big Moment will instantly leave you and be replaced by an overwhelming feeling of pride, joy, and accomplishment. Not to mention you will be surrounded by love from the people with you on this day, your classmates included. Take it all in and embrace all the feelings and memories that these few moments will give you for the rest of your life.

Your classmates, who have stood by you and cheered you on as you read your parashah, will also be reading and might also be nervous on this day. This is why it is very important to give them the same amount of attention and respect as they chant their Torah portion. Provide them with same amount of love that they all bestowed upon you during your moment. Remember how it felt and return it tenfold to your fellow classmates. Just as it meant to you, so it will mean to them to have your love and support as they too become a B-Mitzvah.

After each of your classmates have completed their portions, you will find that the synagogue and congregation will instantly turn from serious and focused to happy and joyful. The rabbi will present you to the congregation as B'nai Mitzvah and you will receive a congregational blessing. The way each congregation conducts their final blessing and "closing ceremonies" depends on the rabbi and synagogue; but no matter what happens, rest assured that it will be spectacular.

On the evening of my Bat Mitzvah, my classmate Susan and I were each called down from the bimah into the congregation where people were invited up to hold a tallit over us. We stood under the tallit and received a song of blessing and prayed with our fellow congregants. I loved this moment. During the service, I felt separated and distant from my friends and family sitting with the congregation. When we were invited to come down and stand under the tallit with our families, friends, and fellow congregants

by our side, I truly felt a remarkable connectedness with everyone present.

I left the evening with an incredible sense of joy and gratitude. I felt more loved than I could ever have imagined. That feeling has remained with me to this day. This is why it is so important for me to share this book with you, so that you too may know the incredible importance of the journey you are about to undertake or are currently in the process of completing. It is so much more than just another religious school class. As you are preparing for your big day, think about all the men and women throughout the centuries who were unable to complete this process due to their gender, age, or the period in history that forced Jewish people to hide their beliefs in fear of persecution. Keep in your heart the children of the Holocaust, who were taken at a young age and were never given the opportunity to become a B-Mitzvah. As you stand with yad in hand and read from the Torah, carry those people in your heart. Carry on the feeling that you will feel on the evening of your B-Mitzvah throughout your life and never let the flame burn out.

So What Happens Now?

Much like graduating from college, getting married or getting to the end of a literary series that has been the center of your life for as long as you can remember, after your B-Mitzvah the notion of *So what happens now?* might be a thought that will be circulating frequently through your head. The good news is that you can continue your Judaic education any way you like. This was something that I pondered over a great deal after I finished the program. So I began to research and ask questions. First, I met my rabbi briefly after Shabbat services and began picking her brain on what I could do to continue reading Hebrew. She was overjoyed at the fact that I wanted to continue learning and reading and said that she would arrange some more opportunities for me to read an aliyah at morning services sometime in the future. A few weeks after that conversation, I received a wonderful email from her asking if I would like to read for High Holy Days, either on Rosh Hashanah or Yom Kippur. I was blown away at that request. I was expecting to read a portion or two during our monthly morning minyans, but I received much more than that. My rabbi had enough faith in me to ask me to perform this task on one of the holiest of days in our Jewish calendar. Like my B-Mitzvah I was nervous, but I was 100% up to the task and accepted.

There are a lot of other things that you can choose to do after you have become a B-Mitzvah. It could be studying with your children or your grandchildren to help them complete their B-Mitzvah, or offering to tutor other adult B-Mitzvah students during breaks in classes.

The whole point of this process is to continue a time-honored tradition of our people and keep the language and words of the Torah alive through the generations. We are commanded to inscribe the words of the Torah on our lips, in our hearts, in our minds, and on our doorposts. We are taught to teach these words to our children and to the world around us. By becoming a B-Mitzvah, you are doing just that. Whether you choose to keep reading and studying Torah, or simply encourage others interested in the program to take the chance and go for it, you are keeping the words of our people alive and thriving.

The reason I chose to write this book is precisely that. It is not easy to take on something like this with your busy work schedule, your children, your grandchildren, or your life in general; it is so much easier to put other things in front of becoming a B-Mitzvah.

It is now your responsibility to continue Judaism in any way that is personal to you. You don't have to go out and join the rabbi on the bimah, you aren't expected to attend each and every Shabbat service, and no one will be upset if you suddenly forget how to read a letter, a word, or a phrase in Hebrew. What is the most important is continuing to spread the importance of the B-Mitzvah to others, and to ensure that this tradition never dies.

When I finished my Bat Mitzvah journey, I still had that desire and longing to continue, and to know and do more. Some of you may feel that way as well, whereas others consider their B-Mitzvah the completion of their studies in Judaism. Both viewpoints are fine; it all depends on your schedule, willingness, and enthusiasm.

Plenty of people, myself included, are aware of how easy it can be to forget your Hebrew when the religious school at your synagogue is on vacation. It is for this reason that considering becoming a tutor is important and will also help you retain the knowledge you gained during your studies. Think about how much more at ease you felt studying with your fellow classmates during school break. Not only did it keep everything fresh in your head, but it also assisted with committing your knowledge of Hebrew to memory. You could contribute so much to the life of a soon-to-be B-Mitzvah and further support the sustainability of Hebrew—the language of our people. These are only some of the things that you can do after you become a B-Mitzvah. However, if becoming a B-Mitzvah was your light at the end of a long tunnel and you feel you have reached the finish line of your education in Judaism, that is okay too! What is most important is that you did it, and you are now a part of a large group of people who have made the commitment to themselves and to their faith.

Conclusion

I hope this book has inspired you to take the next step in your journey and to see it through until the very end. The next section contains first-hand student stories of B-Mitzvah experiences. These stories were written by students throughout the United States. It is my hope that through reading about their journeys you will see that no matter where you are in your life and no matter how busy you feel you are, you too can become a B-Mitzvah. It's never too late to start, and it all begins with you saying *YES!* to Judaism. It is a big step, a big commitment, but I promise that you can do it! Mazel Tov on your journey. I wish you so much joy and happiness in your world and the world of those around you. *Yasher Koach!*

Student Stories

The following section contains first-hand accounts from past B-Mitzvah students from across the United States. The journey to the Torah contains many paths, each one different for every person whose dream it is to one day be called a Bar or Bat Mitzvah, and your journey will be unique too.

As such, you will notice some differences in transliterations and experiences, as each differ from one synagogue to another.

My wish for you is to read these stories when you feel stuck, unmotivated, or in need of inspiration during your journey.

Let your story be a testament to your accomplishment, and as you encounter people whose dream it is too, share your journey with them as inspiration to take that next step, as the following stories will do for you.

Arava Talve
Temple Beth Israel (Pomona, California)

Something happened to me when my oldest son turned four. I realized I needed to make a decision about raising him as a Jew. The man I married was supportive but not a member of the tribe. He was an ex-Catholic who had issues with organized religion. I was the one who was changing, and happily. He understood my need for our children to know more about my Jewish heritage. I pushed myself to the local shul and enrolled Alec in the pre-K program. This sparked something inside of me. I wanted to know more. My parents considered themselves "cultural Jews" and, growing up in the shadow of the Holocaust, they just didn't know or care to know more about being Jewish. They simply knew they were Jewish and that was good enough for them. As my son began his journey, I slowly began mine. I didn't really connect with the rabbi, so I found myself a teacher at the local Hillel. I took Hebrew classes with college students and read books like Heschel's *Shabbat*, several on Kabbalah, and started attending a Torah study. At the time, I was working as a psychologist in the field of family violence. I was a member of the shul and willingly went to High Holy Day services as opposed to being dragged as a kid. The more I learned, the more I wanted to know. I started to question the words and think about their meaning.

After a few years of study, my teacher asked me if I was ready to be called to Torah. Her language was great. It wasn't a question of *if* it was going to happen, but *when*. As an adult, she said, you decide where you want to fall into the Torah. I had been through a few cycles of Torah study, so I was somewhat familiar with our Torah story; so after some wrestling, I chose Beshelach. I chose the shirah, the song of the sea. I chose the portion about taking a leap of faith because that's what I felt like I was doing. Rabbi Devorah was amazing because she guided me as an adult learner. It was a true balance between the keva (the fixed liturgy) and kavanah (the intent). Studying the words, and more importantly, what the words mean to me. I was ready to add my voice to all those that had come before, and she made me feel like I had every right to!

We studied for two years and I continued to learn the siddur, to chant the parasha and the haftarah. I didn't have anything to compare my learning to because I was her only student, so we studied everything. I invited my family and turned my home into a sanctuary. I had three sons by then, so juggling my work, study and family was a true challenge. Becoming a Bat Mitzvah was amazing, and everyone wanted to be present to share my journey.

Two months later I received a call from the local temple. The rabbi had died suddenly, and the B-Mitzvah coordinator was very ill. They needed someone to work with the students and to help where help was needed. How could I say no? Everything changed for me over the next few years. I became the *Melamedet* of the Temple Beth Israel in Pomona and created a new B-Mitzvah program that was based on integrity of learning. The program needed the school to be strong. We all worked together so I would be able to teach the next generation the skills needed to chant from the ancient texts, lead a service and tell us what it all means. Along the way I taught many adults. Classes of men and women, just women, and my favorite—working with individual adults who want to learn it all! My oldest student was a man named Sam Sucherdaler who was 92. He had a stroke while we were studying, and we then had our lessons at the rehabilitation hospital. I've taught women who have converted, women who decided (like me) that they wanted to know more. I am currently working with a famous concert pianist and a group of 8 women who will become B'not mitzvah in January. I loved my journey to Torah so much that I made it my work. Not like I don't use my training in psychology as I work with families during an amazing time in their lives. I taught all three of my sons, a nephew and a few others online, and many children and adults who were called to Torah in Israel.

I think my favorite thing is watching a woman's face when she is called to Torah for the first time. Some of these women were told that the ritual was only for boys. They were kept on the "outside." Being counted and finding your own letter in the Torah is empowering on every level.

I was 36 when I became a Bat Mitzvah. That was 22 years ago, and it was just the beginning of my life as an adult Jewish learner and educator. I have served as a lay leader, led all types of minyans, been the director of education at a shul and taught students of all ages. It's been one of my greatest joys. My three sons all strongly identify as Jews and my oldest is marrying a Jewish woman in September. I am currently the Melamedet at Temple Sinai in Palm Desert. BTW—my husband never converted but continues to be supportive and proud of the path I have chosen.

Gail Erlitz
Congregation Children of Israel (Augusta, Georgia)

Last August 25th (2017), I and 5 other women celebrated our B-Mitzvah. For myself the reason why I did it now at age 62 was that we had a new Israeli rabbi who just sparked the interest and desire to do so. I grew up Jewish but never went to religious school, so I never had a Bat Mitzvah. Other women in our class grew up secular as I did or were raised in an Orthodox home where women did not become Bat Mitzvah. We studied with the rabbi only 5 months and had very short Torah portions (Ekev 20 was mine) but the 6 of us women bonded, and it was a wonderful experience. During service on Friday evening and Saturday morning, each of us women displayed family heirlooms and artifacts of our ancestors. Each of us gave a speech explaining what the experience meant to us. For me, I had just moved my mother from the apartment I grew up in in Queens, New York to a senior independent living house, and in doing so I found photographs of my grandmother's family from Russia/Poland pre-WWII. The family members who remained in Europe all were lost during the Holocaust; so for me, it was reconnecting with my roots. Additionally, each of us obtained the name of a child lost to the Holocaust who never became Bat Mitzvah. As we read from the Torah, each of us said, "I stand here before you along with *Klari Hamosh* (or the name of their child), who perished at age 9 in the Holocaust. Additionally, as we sat on the bimah, next to each of us was an empty chair with a flower, tallit, and their name on the chair and a memorial candle underneath the chair.

A few weeks before the ceremony, we prepared a traditional Jewish dinner for our families. Each of us made a dish (or two) and we feasted on chicken soup with matzo balls, brisket, noodle kugel, kasha varnishkes, chopped liver, rugelach, and apple strudel, just to name a few of the dishes. I made rugelach and the chopped liver—

and even made the schmaltz from scratch! (I remembered watching my mother make it when I was a child!) At the dinner, we showed a few of our family artifacts; this is what gave our rabbi the idea for us to display them at the service. By doing this the rabbi helped us reconnect with the recipes that generations before us had prepared. We realized it is now up to us to keep the traditions going.

Susan Edwards Martin
Temple Beth Hillel (Valley Village, California)

My Jewish journey began when I was born to two wonderful parents, Edith and Harold. They were kind, loving and incredibly supportive. The most important thing to them was family, a key component in Judaism. We went to temple during the holidays and lit Shabbat candles. We'd honor family members who had died with yahrzeit candles and shared stories about them. I was always amazed that when the choir sang "Avinu Malkeinu, Sh'ma kolenu" my mother would invariably cry.

As a little girl, I didn't quite understand why she cried; but now I do. The song resonated in her heart and soul of her deep-rooted passion, love and connectedness to her Jewish upbringing. I got it. I remember on high holy days, we'd get all dressed up and because the temple was so crowded, we'd have to sit in chairs way in the back on a stage. I thought G-d was the Eternal Light and if I focused my eyes on it long enough, I'd feel G-d's presence. I had a sense that G-d lived inside of me and he was my secret and special, magical friend. I also knew at four years old that G-d had a plan for me and I was here to share my joy of singing and entertaining.

My brother Ed became Bar Mitzvah and even though it was expected for boys to have their Bar Mitzvah in the 1950s and 60s, it wasn't as popular for girls. Resigned to the reality, that that's the way it was, I continued my Judaic studies and completed my confirmation in the 10th grade instead.

You may wonder, "Why be a Bat Mitzvah now, at this time in my life?" Why not? I am a firm believer that we are never too old to realize our dreams, and this was one of those dreams for me.

My son Nick was an inspiration when he went through his Bar Mitzvah three years ago, doing such a terrific job, learning all the prayers, reading Hebrew and studying Torah. I'd come to services and hear the prayers and songs but didn't know them as well as everyone else. The entire congregation was singing the beautiful melodies, reciting the prayers with such self-assurance. I soon discovered that most of the women in my Sisterhood here at TBH had all been through their Bat Mitzvah as adults. I wanted to understand what they knew. I wanted to experience and feel totally comfortable with all the music and prayers. I wanted to earn the right and be a proud owner of my own tallit! My son and my sisterhood friends were my inspiration. It was my time to be a B-Mitzvah.

I have always loved being Jewish. I love the traditions, the music, the reverence of family, doing good deeds and mitzvot, Tu BiSh'vat, the respect for trees, nature and the environment, and all of G-d's creations, and of course, matzah ball soup and chocolate chip mandel bread! I love that my husband Peter, who is not Jewish, has been open and accepting of all our Jewish practices in our home as well as at temple. You should hear him say the blessings and sing Bim Bam! We have created a family tradition to light Shabbat candles every Friday night and observe all the Jewish holidays. I feel confident that Nick will continue to pass down our Jewish values and traditions with his family, creating memories of his own and remembering all the things that we did as a family and that he will hold them as near and dear to his heart, as we have done.

Thank you, Peter and Nick, for all your love and support these past two years, encouraging me to follow my dream of becoming a Bat Mitzvah. Thank you, Rabbi Sarah, Cantor Jen and Cantor Shana, for guiding me and showing me the way. Thank you for sharing your passion and knowledge of Judaism. You have inspired me greatly and I appreciate you. Thank you, Chrissie, for sharing this journey with me. You are a delight and I have loved being Bat Mitzvah partners with you. I'm so proud of you and how you embraced all the Hebrew and prayers. I think you are awesome. Thank you, Cousins Patti and Stan, for making the trip from Marin County, to share in the joy of this evening. Thank you to my niece Debbie, for being here along with Patti and Stan, representing our family, and thank you to all of my friends and congregants for joining us this evening. It means the world to me that you are here. I know my mother and father are very pleased that I have embraced my Jewishness and have taken this important and transcendent step in my Jewish growth. I can feel them smiling down and kvelling.

Marc J. Dahlman
Congregation Gates of Prayer (Metairie, Louisiana)

I took Hebrew as a youngster in Indiana, but quickly forgot most of it. Coming from small northern towns, it was not common for a Reform Jew to become Bar Mitzvah.

My non-Jewish wife, Sherene, and I took a one-day course offered by Philip Gaethe and Rabbi Loewy, and we both loved it. Ever since, Sherene usually reads the blessings in Hebrew at home (and sometimes in public!).

In my seventh decade, a year or so later, the thought of expanding my mind, coupled with the desire to read Kaddish at my parents' grave site, clicked when I saw that Philip was teaching a weekly class—he made the learning fun and meaningful.

The subject of B-Mitzvah was raised, and I thought that to be an amazing opportunity. Although only two of us actually finished that year, several others were stimulated by our success and succeeded us the next few years. I'd recommend this to anyone, a self-fulfilling accomplishment.

Geraldine S. Epstein
Bet Aviv (Columbia, Maryland)

On November 19, 2016 at Bet Aviv in Columbia, Maryland, six adults celebrated their combined B'nai Mitzvah, five women and one man. We each led prayers at the Saturday morning service, read from the Torah, from Genesis Chapter 18 or 22, and delivered a speech about the meaning of the day to us to the 300 members of Bet Aviv and guests who came to celebrate our accomplishments. We had studied with Rabbi Bernstein for a little over a year to arrive at that day and most of us learned Hebrew from scratch. We also worked with our cantor, Linda Baer, to learn our Torah portions.

In July 1938, my mother arrived in Hartford, Connecticut for an extended visit with her mother's brother and sister and their families. Little did she know then that when she left Poland, she would never see her parents or 8 brothers and sisters alive again. When I was in kindergarten, my teacher picked me, the only Jewish kid in the school, for the role of Virgin Mary in the school Christmas play. I couldn't understand why my parents were not as excited by this prospect as I was. Three years later, when we moved from East Hartford to Bloomfield, my parents decided it was time to join a synagogue. They chose Beth Hillel, a Conservative synagogue that was just being organized. The first year we belonged, I happily attended Sunday school where we learned Bible stories. A couple of years later, when my parents tried to enroll me in Hebrew school, they were told that I was too old to start Hebrew school with the younger children. I would have to study for a year with private tutor to catch up. Since my parents couldn't afford that extra expense, that was an abrupt halt to my formal religious training. As a result, I always felt lost during the services we attended, since I didn't know the rituals, songs or prayers and couldn't follow the Hebrew.

Now we fast forward to 1975. I'm married with two children

and we joined Temple Isaiah. Although we belonged to Temple Isaiah for more than 25 years, it never felt welcoming to me. When I found myself free to make my own decisions in 2003, I decided that I wanted to find a synagogue that better met my needs. So, I went shul shopping. I came to my first service at Bet Aviv in August of 2003, just before the High Holidays. We met in Amherst House and there were about 3C people at the service. After the service, we moved to the oneg room, formed a circle around the table and held hands for the motzi. This simple act made me feel connected to this warm community. Later in the evening, when Barbara Hurwitz gave me a hug of welcome, I knew that Bet Aviv was the right place for me.

The rest, as they say, is history. I quickly became very active, served on a number of committees, and eventually had leadership roles in the congregation as Secretary, Vice President and Co-President with Marty Stein. During this time, I became a regular Shabbat worshipper. Over time I did learn the rituals, prayers and songs and so filled in some of that Jewish education I missed as a child. But reading Hebrew still proved elusive.

When Rabbi Bernstein announced last year that he would be offering a B-Mitzvah class, I knew right away that I wanted to participate. During the class, when Rabbi Bernstein asked each of us to pick a prayer from the Amidah that we would explore deeply, I picked the Modim prayer. I have been interested in gratitude for some time. Many studies have been conducted about the role of gratitude in our lives and they all come to similar conclusions: people who practice gratitude regularly are happier, healthier and may even live longer. I decided to start a simple Modim practice of my own. When I wake up in the morning, I just simply say, "Thank-you G-d for another day in good health." More recently I've expanded my practice. In the morning I'll think about what I have to do that day and ask for G-d's blessing. If it's a day when I'm coaching students at Howard Community College, I might ask

G-d to inspire me to ask a question that would get that student one step closer to their financial goals. Then in the evening I review what happened that day. I thank G-d for the things that went well, and also for the opportunity to learn from things that could have gone better. In this way, I begin and end my day with a connection to G-d and it makes it me feel good. So, I would encourage each of you to establish a Modim practice of your own. It's something that is easy to do, hardly takes any time and has the benefits of health, happiness and longevity. And, if you do, I'd love to hear from you.

I've always been in awe of people who could read from the Torah and today I'm excited to be doing it myself. Today is the culmination of a lifelong desire to complete some missing pieces of my Jewish education. After my Mom died in 1983, when some important event like a promotion at work would happen to me, my Dad would always say, "Your mother would be so proud of you." Well today, I am proud of myself. And I'm sure both my mother and my father would be proud of me too.

Arlene Greenberg
Reform Temple Beth Shalom (Winter Haven, Florida)

Hi, my name is Arlene. Currently I am a member of Reform Temple Beth Shalom in Winter Haven, Florida. On June 3, 2017, I became Bat Mitzvah with three other women. At 77 years of age, I was the oldest.

Some background information. I grew up in the west side of Chicago in a fairly Orthodox but rapidly changing neighborhood. I walked to Hebrew school four days a week. No school on Friday. On Saturday, there were services for the children in a different part of the shul, while the adults remained in the main part. Sunday was Sunday school. My parents never forced me to go to Hebrew school. I went because from the beginning, I enjoyed learning, even though back then I was always the youngest. Now I am the oldest. I remember thinking that the Abraham in the Bible was Abraham Lincoln the past president.

When my family moved to Florida, we belonged to a conservative synagogue. I was married in that synagogue. Many years later, after my husband passed away, I moved to Winter Haven, Florida to be closer to my younger son. What a surprise to find a Reform temple in a relatively non-Jewish area. As soon as I walked into the synagogue, I felt welcomed. The congregants stopped what they were studying, and after finding out that my husband recently passed away, said the Kaddish with me. It doesn't matter whether a synagogue is Orthodox, Conservative, or Reform, the prayers are the same, and as a people there is a connection.

Which brings me to the Bat Mitzvah. The four of us could read Hebrew and never thought about having one until it was a thought that grew and grew. Why not, if the boys could do it, why not the girls of any age? Our wonderful Rabbi, Garson Herzfeld, encouraged us to proceed.

My eldest son was on a visit to Israel with his family. He purchased my very special tallit. During the ceremony, my youngest son wrapped the tallit around me as did the other children in the B'not Mitzvot group.

At first, I was going to perform the ceremony, because I could, and it seemed like fun. But as I studied further, I became interested in learning to read from our Torah (which is more difficult than just reading Hebrew with the vowels). Our portion was the book of Ruth and we each took a section. Mine was Ruth. Another was the Ten Commandments. Another was Naomi, and finally, the significance of the tallit and the importance of charity.

It was a learning experience. We each wrote a meaningful speech and spoke to a temple full of people. It was decided that none of us needed or wanted gifts, but that a donation would be helpful (part of which would go to the temple, and the other part would help women in need).

It was a very successful event. The rabbi was very helpful in organizing and helping us learn our portions.

Next year other people may be willing to go forward with their own Bat Mitzvah. We hope it will become a yearly event. In the meantime, our Sunday school is teaching non-readers the Hebrew letters and several prayers.

I love being Jewish and having a connection to a wonderful synagogue.

Shelly Welfeld
Temple Sinai (Stamford, Connecticut)

Each of us is on a journey and today I'd like to share a bit about mine.

I was brought up in a traditional modern Orthodox home, and I went to bicultural day school through 8th grade. As a child, I remember walking 2.5 miles to services on the High Holy Days. We mostly kept Shabbat: no cooking, no shopping, and no driving. I knew all of the liturgy by heart. I learned to read and write Hebrew alongside English as part of my everyday studies. As my 13th birthday approached, I was given the choice—did I want to become a Bat Mitzvah? Well, there was no way I going to get up in front of my peers and lead a worship service, let alone write a sermon. Nevertheless, on a girl's 13th birthday one automatically becomes a Bat Mitzvah. But as Rabbi Jay explained to us in our very first class, that on the day of your 13th birthday we automatically became a Bar/Bat Mitzvah, which was something I knew, but I never really understood what that meant. So, what does it mean to become a Bat Mitzvah? We tell our children when they are 13, that in the eyes of the Jewish law they are now considered to be adults and are responsible for their own actions. Today as I become a Bat Mitzvah a bit older than 13, I am reaffirming and deepening my commitment to Judaism.

My father passed away a little more than 5 years ago, and since his passing I have been on a spiritual journey of sorts. During the first year, I attended almost every Friday night service here at Temple Sinai in order to say Kaddish for him, and on Saturday mornings, I attended a Modern Orthodox service at Beit Chaverim in Westport, alongside my mother, to support her and to worship, say Kaddish and mourn with my parents' community as well.

Wavering between the two, I was not really sure where I belonged. Despite my uncertainty, however, I felt a very comforting spiritual presence leading me and guiding me along my journey. And, ultimately, bringing me to this moment here today.

I had been considering becoming an adult Bat Mitzvah here at Temple Sinai for many, many years and last summer I decided that the time was right. I was still not sure why, but I knew that it was time for me to take on the task of deepening my knowledge and connection to Judaism. Maybe I felt grounded in my life and ready to take on the next chapter, so to speak, or maybe it was an excuse for the new dress and heels!

Today, in addition to being Shabbat Parasha Korach (the weekly portion of Korach), it is also Shabbat Rosh Chodesh — the renewal of the moon which marks the beginning of a new month of the Jewish calendar. When I realized that "our" Shabbat was also Rosh Chodesh, I asked the rabbi and cantor if I could read the separate portion that is read on every Rosh Chodesh. I asked not to be difficult or special, but because I wanted to share in the meaning of why Rosh Chodesh is important to me.

According to our tradition, the celebration of Rosh Chodesh, a specifically feminine observance, was given to the women of Israel as a reward because they refused to surrender their gold when the Israelites were forging the Golden Calf at the base of Mount Sinai. Because of their righteous act, women are traditionally excused from working on Rosh Chodesh. The holiday is also meaningful to us as women because our bodies and monthly cycles are intrinsically tied to the cycles of the moon—so which came first?

On a visit to Israel about 3½ years ago, I had the incredible experience of being able to attend a Women of the Wall Rosh Chodesh service in Jerusalem. W.O.W.'s mission is to attain social and legal recognition of women's rights: our right to wear a tallit, to pray, and to read from the Torah, collectively and aloud, at the Western Wall—something that is still forbidden today. I was moved to tears as I sang and prayed with my sisters at the Wall, but I also felt their pain at not being able to read from an actual Torah.

Throughout the history of the Jewish people, our flame has waxed and waned, just like the phases of the moon. But even in the depth of darkness, the flame of Jewish hope has never been extinguished.

For me, personally, these past few years have been very challenging, but I kept moving forward. I always try to find the silver lining of the dark storm cloud, always try to find the positive in a difficult situation. Through the support of some very close friends, my Temple Sinai and my Beit Chaverim family, I have persevered through it all.

Much like I told my own children at their B'nai Mitzvah, I know this day marks a new beginning for me on my Jewish journey. Through it all, I have learned that it is never too late to begin again. And I believe it was *bashert* (or meant to be) that this Rosh Chodesh begins the month of Tammuz—the month which marks the beginning of summer, my favorite season and the best possible time I could imagine to begin this next leg of my journey.

So, where do I belong? As long as I am thankful to G-d and express gratitude for the blessings in my life, I am exactly where I belong. And today, on Rosh Chodesh Tammuz, it is my honor and privilege to know that my Bat Mitzvah sisters and I are adding our voices to the chorus of the Women of the Wall singing and chanting our ancient prayers and striving to make their place in the world, and find their path forward on their Jewish journeys. I hope and pray that in the not-too-distant future, Jewish women everywhere will find their voices and be free to speak and sing aloud in every Jewish community.

Robin S. Kay
Beit Haverim (Lake Oswego, Oregon)

I was a member of the 2015 adult B-Mitzvah class at Beit Haverim in Lake Oswego, Oregon. When it was time for me to start Bat Mitzvah training, my father was unwilling to drive me to Hebrew classes. It was okay for my brother to go four years earlier; but I was and still am a girl.

I taught a religious school class for 10 years, for the five-, six- and seven-year-old students. One of the things I taught them was their Hebrew letters. I learned my letters along with them. I thought it was a good idea to start them learning as soon as possible.

After my children became B-Mitzvah, I read several times from the Torah during High Holiday Services. My daughter was a very good tutor. My mother had purchased a tallis for me, which I wore proudly. I had often led Shabbat Services, both for the children and the adult service. But sometimes I felt like a fraud because I had not had my own Bat Mitzvah service.

I decided that it was finally my time to go through the whole ceremony. I needed to prove to myself that I could do it. I taught myself the letters I hadn't learned with my students (for some reason, mostly the vowels) and practiced a lot.

My class had four other women in it. I was by far the youngest. We had relatively similar stories about not becoming Bat Mitzvah at the usual age. We were an incredible group with diverse backgrounds who formed a special bond that still exists to this day. Going through the adult B-Mitzvah experience has given me a lot more confidence.

I am currently studying my Torah portion, preparing to once more read it on Yom Kippur. I stand proudly by the Torah as I am now a Bat Mitzvah.

Mike B.
Bet Aviv (Columbia, Maryland)

I was the only adult male in Rabbi Seth Bernstein's B-Mitzvah 2016 class with 5 women (Sept 2015-Sept 2016).

Why and life journey...
(Below is not from my 2016 B-Mitzvah speech.)

I was age 69 in 2016, born in 1947 to second generation Jewish parents who were not observant, never affiliated, each from Jewish parents but also from broken homes as children (loss of a parent through death or divorce). At age 4, I remember my dad telling my older brother and me we were Jewish, and I remained proud of that ever since.

We attended our relatives' Jewish marriages and Bar Mitzvahs in New Jersey, so I knew about most of typical American Jewish customs by junior high. Some of my older relatives spoke a little Yiddish to me: "Mike, so *Nu?*"

While I started Sunday school at age 6, there was no commitment by my parents to see it continue; we moved four times by fifth grade into non-Jewish communities.

And I rebelled at the elimination of weekend playtime outdoors for the short period I attended Sunday school. We lived near deep woods, a railroad, and a marina in Havre de Grace, Maryland from 1947-1953.

Also, I do not remember my parents ever explaining why I was going to Sunday school, nor from our Sunday school instructor.

I tried to locate the 1953 Sunday school in Harford County, Maryland in 2016 by Google and the current temple, and found that they probably rented an American Legion hall or school.

My two brothers (older and younger) did not seek Bar Mitzvah nor remain Jewish when it came to marriage; I am the only one.

My sister converted because all her friends were Christian.

As a high school senior in a non-Jewish community (Catonsville, Maryland), my Jewish gene erupted. I needed to find a way back to a more Jewish life. While the Christian students were OK, I found a bit of anti-Semitism from their parents while dating a little in high school. That was my cue to actively pursue a new course. I would not repeat what my parents did. We moved near a Jewish community in Baltimore County 1965 when I was 18. That was a good but late start. It was near a large, famous pool/quarry (Milford Mill Pool) which only a few years prior had a sign, *No Dogs or Jews* and was in the movie Cry Baby (You know, Johnny Depp and Hatchet-face). I worked at a Jewish resort in the Poconos for the summers of 1965 and 1966; wonderful experience and it paid for half my college costs.

As a 1965 college engineering freshman (College Park, 20% Jewish, 10,000 residing on campus with classes swelling to 30,000 daily from commuters), my roommate for one semester was an affable senior in Agriculture and a very religious Christian. I would come back from classes to find people kneeling in front of my bed and praying to Jesus; so, I would just come back later. I could do my homework in a common room or at the library. And yes, he tried to convert me to Christianity because he saw I was weak in Judaism, and stressed Jesus was the only bridge to salvation. I did attend one of the campus' Christian meetings at his request and out of a tiny bit of curiosity, and I was completely underwhelmed and looked for the exit to escape. Thank you, Jesus, for letting me escape.

(This reminds me of the daily prayer readings from the New Testament in Maryland elementary schools before the pledge of allegiance. When it was my turn to read the prayer, they were just words. Please G-d, let me be delivered from the New Testament.)

I tried to learn Hebrew on campus in 1965, but the Hillel rabbi did not want to start at the beginning even though his course was entitled Beginning Hebrew. In front of the class he said my

Hebrew knowledge did not match the average, and asked me to leave. As I was walking out I asked the students (all female) "is this what you want?" and all I heard was silence (crickets). I still have the book (Modern Hebrew, Blumberg). I don't think Hebrew was available as a college course then.

In the 1980s my wife and I attended a Hebrew class with Rabbi Kumin in Columbia, Maryland, and later joined another class where Rabbi Noah Golinkin and his wife taught us to read Hebrew during Sunday meetings at classmate homes from a book he published that was also used in the religious school for children. Then my wife and I joined Temple Isaiah in Columbia, Maryland and its choir. I stayed in the choir for over 15 years. My wife stayed longer. At Temple Isaiah, when we joined, the rule was you must volunteer for something, so the choir became our standard. We loved singing the Hebrew prayers and melodies. My favorites were those arranged by Debbie Friedman and Craig Taubman.

So, learning Hebrew was revisited in the 2016 B-Mitzvah class. Having 4 years of Latin in junior/high school, one semester of Russian in post-college studies, I was able to read and pronounce Hebrew easily with the teaching from our rabbi and previous rabbis. I chose to join the class because I wanted to learn. I was retired in 2013, the number of classmates was adequate (barely a minimum), meeting times and location were easy, and my wife urged me. The rabbi held a first meeting to share an outline of the class. There were a few dropouts at the beginning and a few during; six remaining. I was ready for the B-Mitzvah in three months, but the class was originally slated to last 13 months (too long). I am not a writer and worse yet, not a public speaker. I was hoping I could perform what was necessary privately among the five with only my wife as an invitee. Instead, we held our invited guests down to about 40, and over 325 total guests attended the November 19, 2016 B-Mitzvah Saturday service. My mouth went dry. All six of us were to read a small portion of the Torah for the second day of Rosh Hashanah—the Akedah/the Binding of Isaac/Genesis 22. The service before and after Torah was also divided, and spreadsheeted with cues, so we could rehearse speaking, and holding and walking with the Torah. We all read one Hebrew learning book, *Aleph Isn't Tough* (Motzkin) at our own pace, and I read a second, Learn Hebrew Today (Yedwab) that the rabbi also provided. Even with these newer books, you need a rabbi to make it work. I found another rabbi Torah chanter on YouTube (Rabbi Weisblum) who helped me chant my portion Genesis 22:16-18. I also chanted the Kedushah; and chanted part of Psalm 92 with the Bet Aviv cantor who plays the guitar wonderfully. Having listened to very few adult Bar Mitzvahs on the web, I knew our practice made us better. A side note for the web: I feel Judaism on the web needs to be more than significantly improved both in content, organization and searching. During 2016, I read part of the Tanakh, having never fully read the Old Testament, but I read each of the Five books of Moses backwards in English, starting with Deuteronomy, so I could check any foreshadowing. Having done that, I don't recommend reading them backwards, because the foreshadowing wasn't that difficult. I photographed our Torah scroll portions with a cellphone and emailed them to the classmates; the Torah fonts are slightly different than what was provided to us on paper. Our class donated siddurs (*Mishkan Tefilah*) to Bet Aviv, and we were awarded a book of our choosing; I selected *Start-up Nation* (Senor, Singer) The six of us were invited to repeat our Torah portions on Rosh Hashanah, Thursday September 21, 2017, and I chanted Genesis 22:16-19.

Long before I was married, a rabbi let me know it was all right not to worry about being a Bar Mitzvah; he said I was already a Bar Mitzvah, and to go about my life. But what he missed was being taught Jewish history, law, customs, and life from rabbinical viewpoints. You don't find that explained well and concisely in any book or on the web.

Married in 1974, my wife and I affiliated in the 1980s first at Temple Isaiah (Reform) in Columbia, Maryland, then Bet Aviv in 2012. We really did not "change" temples, because Bet Aviv resulted from a split from Isaiah over establishing a new building of their own, or remaining in a shared worship center (interfaith centers) with Christian congregations. Our two girls, born 1977 and 1980, attended Jewish day care (Bet Yeladim), then Hebrew school (Temple Isaiah), Jewish summer day camps (Milldale), became B'not Mitzvah, and were also confirmed. We attended many of their friends' Bar/Bat Mitzvah services. Our younger daughter attended a pre-birthright BZD trip to Israel in 1997. We were charter members of the D.C. Holocaust Museum and Philadelphia American Jewish History Museum. My wife grew up in and around Carteret, New Jersey, and had an Orthodox Bat Mitzvah. But the Orthodox community changed to Conservative over time. Her many relatives there were pillars in the Jewish community. We visited them frequently and attended their Seders and reunions (and shivas) while our girls were growing up. We chose the Reform congregation in Columbia because many of our Jewish friends were there. I feel Columbia really has one virtual roof for all Howard County Jews, affiliated or not. I took it for granted that Howard County has had a strong Jewish community. I learned of Rouse's "city" growing in the woods and farmlands in an area east and west of Route 29, halfway between Baltimore and Silver Spring in the late 1960s. Our second home (1978) there was near woods, and surprisingly I could hear owls and see some chickens running in the woods from a small farm I never sought. Across our two cul-de-sac streets were remnants of a farm from the 1700s—two silos, a barn renovated for renters, a woodhouse, a buried concrete floor.

A year after college—1971—I was lucky to meet my future wife at D.C. coffee houses and dances sponsored by Adas Israel and the Rockville JCC. Many of my college friends married during college. Remember Operation Match? That was fun for finding

Jewish friends, but no marriage partner. I raised the education bar as I met Jewish ladies. I felt most comfortable with women who were well educated (master's degree or better) and established in a profession. Remember, there was no internet then, and Jewish life on campus was ironically very small for such a large Jewish population (1965-70), and with a Hillel that was largely dark.

After college, my dad let me know that while he was in Patton's 3rd Army he saw the ovens and the mountain of ashes at a liberated concentration camp in 1945 where a 15-year-old Eli Weisel survived. In 1945, my dad was 25. He rarely talked about the Holocaust. While watching the movie *Patton* in 1970 with my dad, he didn't even tell me he was in their ranks. He died in 2002 at the age of 82. I did not tell him that America was attacked on 9/11. He survived the Ardennes Battle of the Bulge. I commemorated him in the WWII D.C. Memorial, and the future Fort Belvoir Army Museum. His highest rank was master sergeant, and I remember seeing the big number 3 on his sleeve along with many ribbons on his uniform. Dad took up boxing in the Army; that helped him take care of a few anti-Semitic remarks. I was a late learner of the Holocaust—high school world history. In my fourth year of Latin class, I realized the first Nazis were the Romans. I felt nauseated that I was studying Roman anything. (The Roman Colosseum was built by 20,000 (or more) Jewish slaves paraded in a Roman victory march at the time of the Diaspora. Temple Mount silver and gold paid the bill. The Arch of Titus records the event. Thank you, Rome, for showing us your vileness; please return the stolen artifacts.

While adult B-Mitzvahs were offered frequently at Temple Isaiah (Reform), being a father with constant overtime work due to a reduced workforce, I expected to delay a B-Mitzvah perhaps even up to retirement. Even knowing I was Jewish, my team leader at work had no problem assigning me work during Yom Kippur. Just the opposite for Christmas: people vacationed for a week and their required work usually waited. One time, one of my work leaders followed a non-Jewish coworker to the hospital with a laptop to complete an assignment at his hospital bed less than 24 hours after he was admitted. (Is there any group who will stand up against the new American slavery? Overworked and unbalanced work life.)

But, Rabbi Seth Bernstein's class gave me one more chance. It did fill an indescribable hole in my soul. The learning and preparation was something I could easily do with the class. I loved the history. We learned at an adult level, and shared parts of the service. Thank you, Rabbi Bernstein.

If I were to judge whether a Bar Mitzvah is better as an adult or age 13, no doubt a young age is better. It gives you experiences that you can use for a lifetime. It influences your career choices. That said, I doubt that youths can fully understand the complexities in Torah, Talmud, and from Jewish authors, because we had problems understanding them on an adult level. My wife and I attend weekly Jewish learning at a Lunch and Learn with our rabbi.

We toured Israel for the first time in 2015, a year prior to the B-Mitzvah. I was astonished how Roman the ancient cities are; how peaceful and green the Golan Heights. I loved the artwork, particularly in Safed. Our guide was a tank commander. I learned that the Jordan River, Sea of Galilee and Dead Sea are the same waterway. Wowed by the cities of Tel Aviv and Haifa. The nighttime music video documentary projected on the walls of King David's Citadel was stunning. Our tour applauded the young IDF soldiers whenever we found them, because they were touring as well during a Jewish holiday, and we often met at the same sites. Stuck my feet in the Jordan River with some small fish south of the Sea of Galilee. Great tasting falafels and salads. Marveled that bikes on Tel Aviv's beach promenade were electrified with a lithium battery and a concealed rear axle electric motor. I left a rolled-up note at the Kotel, asking for world peace. At some nonmilitary walking checkpoint, some young man asked if I was Jewish. I said don't I look Jewish? He said no.

When we returned home, I studied the layout of Jerusalem's walled city from pictures of their large model, and created a photo book of the tour.

Marilyn Gaethe
Congregation Gates of Prayer (Metairie, Louisiana)

I became Bat Mitzvah at the ripe old age of 62, in May of 2003. My teacher was my son, Philip Gaethe R.J.E. He is the educator at Congregation Gates of Prayer—to be more accurate, it was a B-Mitzvah service for three ladies and one gentleman, all of us well up in age.

I distinctly remember my father trying to teach me the Hebrew alphabet when I was about seven years old, and him saying to me (in frustration), "Girls just can't learn Hebrew!" Since we lived in England, and knew only Orthodox Judaism, that was that!

Fast forward some 50 years—I am married, living in New Orleans, have two sons, and belong to a Reform synagogue! My son Philip became the educator, obtained his Master's Degree in Jewish Studies through Spertus Institute for Jewish Learning and Leadership and was awarded the designation R.J.E. (Reform Jewish Educator) which is only given to those who have been nominated by their peers. The first time he mentioned the class *Hebrew for Adults*, I signed up! He had no problem teaching his mother—in fact I think he really enjoyed it! I also had to have the cooperation of my husband to chauffer me to lessons every Wednesday for approximately nine months.

To cut a long story short, May came. I had a wonderful B-Mitzvah service, and when I gave my D'var Torah, at the end, I looked up to the heavens and said, "See Dad, girls *can* learn Hebrew!" much to the amusement of everyone there, as I had told them of my father's dismissal of female learning capabilities!

Joanne Wertz
Temple Beth Torah (Chantilly, Virginia)

(Taken from her Bat Mitzvah speech) ...Good evening and thank you all for being here to support Gerald and me for our big endeavor. We have so many people to thank for helping us get to this point. First, I would like to thank my mom, Evelyn Linchuck, who passed away when I was 13 years old. When she drove me to Shaare Tefilah one Tuesday afternoon in September, she looked at me and said, "You don't want to go, do you?" I said, "no," and we drove back home. My parents had hired a tutor, and if I had continued, I wouldn't be here today. I don't think I would have truly appreciated what it meant to read from the Torah at age 13.

My thank yous are very long but heartfelt. Thanks to Rabbi Block for all your support and encouragement. You never made us feel that we couldn't do this, and you offered a lot of support to make this happen.

Sylvia couldn't be here tonight, but she taped our Torah portions and checked in periodically, so we could read the portion over the phone. I loved calling her because she always told me I was fantastic.

I also had support from Jen Harding who took time to sit with me and go over my portion. She found parts I didn't know and really drove them in to me. Jen, you are a great teacher. You don't know how your homework really helped me.

My biggest slave driver was Jamie Wertz. I'm sure it was because we were always on her when it was her Bat Mitzvah year more than six years ago. She put me on a schedule of 30 minutes per day. Thanks Jamie; it really helped.

I just want to say I didn't realize how great all of our kids were because they had three aliyot plus a Haftarah and all the other prayers. We should all be proud. I have never been prouder of my two daughters because I know how many other activities they had going on while preparing. But girls, I hope you are proud of your Mommy because I did it 45 years later. It was hard but so worth it. I now want to continue to learn Hebrew and maybe one day read during High Holidays.

I also want to thank Lori, Kathleen, Danielle and Jamie for making sure the service would go on without a hitch. I really want to thank Mary Horner for all of her work on the program and making sure we got in all of our important parts of the service. And all of my TBT family went together to surprise me on my birthday with the amazing party that will follow this service.

Now I can bring you my message about my Torah portion. Oh wait, I forgot one more thank-you. My wonderful husband who also would say, "You don't want to get up there and embarrass yourself do you? I am not the one up there so you better practice." Oh, I heard Danielle say that too. Hey, like father like daughter. So, I guess that is what I needed. Thanks, Darcy.

Now my portion. It basically has blessings and curses. If you do what G-d wants, you are blessed with good things and if you don't, there will be curses. Well, I think what G-d did in my life was hand me things that seem like curses but turn into blessings. Everyone has tragedy, but I am willing to play Tragedy Poker with any of you, except the rabbi. I think I could win every time. You cannot dwell on what has happened to you throughout your life or you will never be happy or healthy.

My mom died when I was 13 and my dad died when I was 26. My child care provider died six months after my mom. My dog was taken away after my mom died. My boyfriend died. My stepmother died. Two really good friends died young. And I got breast cancer in my lymph nodes.

But we all have tragedy. Each one is different and real to you, but your job is to turn them into blessings. After my mom died, I received Esther when my dad remarried. Then I had two amazing girls who would not have been here without an amazing dad. So, I married late because maybe I had to go through my first longtime relationship ending so I could meet Darcy. I mean you have to make or at least try to make any tragedy into a blessing.

My girlfriends tease me because it never fails that I begin a story and they say, "Does someone die in this story?" Yes, someone usually does. But I wouldn't change any of these relationships. I was given so much in their short lives. These weren't just acquaintances either.

I know as we get older we will all experience more death, but I used to wonder why G-d gave me all this death to experience so early. Maybe because I could handle it. I am just like everyone else. I have moments in my life that are still sad. Memories. We all have bad days or moments of memories. These curses (as some would call them) are blessings to me because I have all these memories to share with you. The people I have lost took care of me in some way that I needed. So now, don't be afraid to be friends with me. Too late, you are stuck with me and not just as an acquaintance. Sorry, you are in.

The rabbi gave a sermon once that has always stayed with me. He said that G-d is in all of your relationships and since my cancer diagnosis, I definitely have remembered that, and I so believe that. Each one of my personal relationships has included G-d in all of them.

Thank you for being here today and sharing in my experience of reading the Torah and making my relationship with G-d stronger.

Michelle Polk
Temple Beth Chaim (Princeton Junction, New Jersey)

Two years ago, upon temple shopping in our new location of Monroe Township, I made an appointment to speak with Rabbi Adena Blum from Temple Beth Chaim in Princeton Junction and share some things that I was looking for in a new congregation. My husband and I had been members of Temple Beth Am in Parsippany for almost 35 years. When we joined our Parsippany congregation we were rather the oddity, since it was before we had children.

One of my desires was a B-Mitzvah class; I was offered the choice years ago, but I declined. As a new rabbi, Rabbi Blum was willing to satisfy my request. Once this was open to this congregation, 25 other members decided to join our class. It was a wonderful experience for us all; we studied for a year and met weekly. Our service was a shared responsibility and we all were grateful to Rabbi Blum for providing us this enriching experience.

Simone H.
Temple Beth Or (Raleigh, North Carolina)

Why Am I Becoming B-Mitzvah, and What It Means to Me Now

I turned 50, and gave myself the gift of freedom to live and grow without inhibition. The buck stops here. I want to make informed choices about my religion/practice and be able to communicate them to others. I want to take responsibility for my own knowledge and choices.

My husband and I had the privilege of going to Israel to celebrate my 50th birthday and our 25th anniversary. It was transformative. Despite being foreigners, we felt a tremendous sense of belonging and connection to our land of origin. When we went to the Wall on Shabbat, as the sun was setting, people of all ages came together spontaneously, freely, and were openly celebrating who we are, and our right to be there. Throughout history, we've had to fight for this privilege, and I stand on their shoulders.

At a TBO dinner, Rabbi Dinner planted the seed, suggesting that I might like becoming a Bat Mitzvah.

Where I am now?

After committing each Wednesday for two years, I have begun to appreciate and the richness of the Hebrew language whose roots and meanings went beyond anything I could have appreciated when I was younger. Our learning included enriching religious and philosophical conversations, which has inspired me to want to learn more. My learning has culminated in my ability to participate in services in a meaningful way, and my sense of accomplishment will always be with me.

Timothy Crouch
Beth Haverim Shir Shalom (Mahwah, New Jersey)

The timing was right... I converted to Judaism just before I got married to Elise. I did not have to convert to get married. The rabbi who did the wedding asked how we planned to raise the children (we didn't have any at the time) and he asked how I felt about converting. My answer was, "If my kids are going to be Jewish, I need to know as much as I can about Judaism."

After all my kids became B'nai Mitzvah, I felt it was my turn/ time to be a Bar Mitzvah. It took a year to get others interested. Eight women and I completed two years of study. We compiled a booklet with each of our stories of our Jewish journey.

I am proud to say we all had an amazing day as we led the service and read from the Torah. We did it! As a side note, I have been attending Torah study for 10 years, learning the Hebrew. I have a personal need to feel I am a part of this community.

Evelyn Rosen
Congregation Emanu El B'nai Jeshurun
(River Hills, Wisconsin)

My synagogue, Congregation Emanu El B'nai Jeshurun, is a Reform synagogue in River Hills, Wisconsin, a suburb of Milwaukee. I have been a member for over 45 years. Rabbi Marc Berkson introduced the Anshe Mitzvah program and I was in the temple's second class.

I was raised in an Orthodox family where I was enrolled in Sunday school & Hebrew School (twice weekly), but was not allowed to read from Torah or become Bat Mitzvah. I was in my late 60s about 13 or 14 years ago when I decided to become Bat Mitzvah.

I was a grandmother of nine at the time and happily, my husband, three children & their spouses and grandchildren supported my decision. I then embarked on a two-year intensive learning program with nine other people. We met once a week. I am able to say unequivocally that this was one of the most rewarding learning programs I have undertaken in my life and of which I am most proud (including my PhD in clinical psychology). I was fortunate to have excellent and patient teachers: Rabbi Bergson and Cantor Barash (who was also then director of lifelong learning).

I was aware that this had been missing in my life despite other accomplishments. I now have a greater understanding and appreciation of the services and their meaning. I have also been honored to chant Torah on Yom Kippur morning for the past dozen or so years. I also chant Torah on the first day of Pesach. As an added bonus, the five remaining members of our class try to meet for lunch a few times a year.

Francine Kolin
East End Temple (New York, New York)

I was raised Orthodox on the lower east side of Manhattan. My brothers, three years older and three years younger, both became Bar Mitzvah in our Orthodox shul. When I was about 12, my dad asked me if I was interested in becoming Bat Mitzvah. Although the shul didn't do that kind of thing, my dad would have arranged for me to maybe read the haftarah, or do something during the service. But I wasn't interested. I had my eye on a Sweet 16, and I knew it was either/or, because our family tradition was a big reception the weekend following a Bar Mitzvah. And I had only had two years of a really crappy Hebrew School, so I didn't really feel excited about that possibility.

Years go by. (My Sweet 16 was awesome, with a live band!) I basically marry the boy next door, the older brother of one of my best friends, two weeks after I graduate from college. We go on a honeymoon, driving from New York City to Niagara Falls in our new car. On the way, we talk about who will light candles at our son's Bar Mitzvah. He is born four years later. We have two children: a boy, and three years later, a girl. Our home is happy with Jewish tradition. We have seders at my parents' house in the Orthodox tradition—start on page one and go to the very end; and seders at my in-law's house—a 15-minute read, and a big dinner. We have mezuzahs on every door. When he turns six, we want to start our son in religious school, but know very well that we are not Orthodox or even Conservative Jews. We are Reform Jews. The way we understood it is that we should choose those things that are meaningful in our Jewish life, and do them. We go to services most every Friday night, and as each child gets into first grade, they come too.

Again, those darn years go by. We are active at our synagogue, East End Temple in New York City. My husband and I both sit on the Board of Trustees. I become President of Sisterhood. Our rabbi starts talking about an adult Hebrew class. Our son becomes a Bar Mitzvah. My husband builds a platform for him to stand on, so we can see him behind the bimah. He reads from Torah, reads the Haftarah, and gives a speech that makes me cry. I am so proud! I think about taking the Hebrew class. But I decide to wait until after our daughter's Bat Mitzvah. She is also wonderful, and starts thinking about becoming a rabbi.

I start the Hebrew class with another congregant, and the rabbi informs us that it will lead to an adult Bat Mitzvah in two years. I improve my Hebrew reading, and the time comes for me to get my Torah portion. Unlike the kids, it isn't connected to my birthday, but is the very last possible Shabbat in the temple calendar in June. I study. I study. I study. I learn the trope that goes along with my portion. I write a speech. I buy a dress. And my day comes. I had been up on the bimah before, had carried the Torah in my role as Sisterhood President lots of times. But this time, I was called up by MY Hebrew name. I actually got a chill, and felt the joy right down to my toes. I watched as they opened the Torah to my portion of the parasha. I sang it out, and it went so well. And I got to make a speech. I spoke about the unfairness of Moses not getting to go into the Promised Land, eventually accepting that we aren't supposed to know all parts of G-d's plans. And at the end... "Not every Bat Mitzvah girl gets to thank her parents AND her children, her rabbi AND her husband."...and so on.

My daughter actually became a rabbi, currently at Central Synagogue in New York City.

Kate Scheinman
Temple Beth El (Dubuque, Iowa)

When my husband, Larry, was offered a job transfer to Dubuque, Iowa, I literally didn't know where Iowa was. Picture the Saul Steinberg *New Yorker* cartoon of a New Yorker's conception of the world: Beginning on Manhattan's West Side, we look west over the Hudson River, bordered by New Jersey, then a rectangle (which includes Chicago and LA), then the Pacific Ocean, bordered by China, Japan, and Russia. So where was Iowa? I was well-traveled: I had studied and lived in Italy; traveled throughout Western Europe; visited East Africa with my Uncle Bill and our adopted Kenyan family; toured with an adult choir in Nicaragua during the Sandinista times; and lived in Sydney, Australia for nearly six years. But Iowa?

So, I did what many of us have done: I went online and found that, yes, there was a temple in Dubuque. Larry and I came out for a visit in February of 1997 (not the most scenic time of year in the Midwest), and had the pleasure of visiting Randy and Rina in their lovely home.

Kate to Randy: "And what do you do?"

Randy: "I am a meat broker."

Kate: "Oh, I am a vegetarian."

When we moved here, Ben was nearly seven and Emily had just turned four. Living in New Jersey and working in New York, Larry and I had not felt the need to join a temple; Jewish life (and our families) were all around us. But moving to Dubuque—with very, very few Jews and no family other than the four of us (and our newly adopted puppy, Daisy)—we immediately joined the temple and went to a temple picnic within a few weeks of moving here. And so, our lives in Dubuque and as part of Temple Beth El began.

For many years, I thought of temple membership as something we were doing for the kids—so that they would have the opportunity to learn about Judaism in the midst of the Christian community. And how well that has turned out for our children: Ben spent 11 months studying at Tel Aviv University after a wonderful exposure to Israel on a Birthright trip. During the school year, Ben works one day a week at Temple Beth Israel in Skokie, and during the summers he works with campers with special needs at our URJ camp, OSRUI. And Emily: her Jewish resume is impressive: President of the Student Board of Hillel at Bradley University; working as a religious school teacher at Congregation Anshai Emeth in Peoria; and when she was in high school, Emily participated in a program of American and Israeli teens working on service projects in both Israel and the U.S. Both Ben and Emily have absorbed the spirit of Tikkun Olam (repairing the world) and plan to live their lives on that path: Ben, as a psychotherapist working with adolescents; and Emily as a social worker—advocating for disability rights.

So, imagine my surprise when I realized that temple Beth El meant much more to me than just a place for my kids. Beth El has become a home for me; a place where I started to feel my own Jewish identity expand; a family to support Larry and me far from our biological families; a group of people who welcome my frequent announcements about our children's accomplishments; a place where—for many years—I have had the honor of chanting the Kol Nidre prayer on Erev Yom Kippur; a group of friends and family who have become a part of my own Jewish Journey.

I am good with languages and at one time or another, I spoke Italian, French, and Spanish. With a little practice, I could get there again. But I am having a heck of a time learning to read Hebrew. When I had the pleasure of visiting Ben in Tel Aviv, I started to pick up some words (*Manishma? Tov tov*), but in my aged brain (or whatever), I find it excruciating to learn to decode the Hebrew letters. I am musical, and probably because of that influence, I learned many of the Shabbat prayers (songs) by heart. I could probably have led an entire service—in Hebrew—but without reading the Hebrew words or understanding what I was saying.

So, I felt stuck in how to move forward, until I spoke with Rabbi Ann. I explained that I wanted to learn more about the prayers, to deepen my understanding of the service, but that learning to read Hebrew was a major stumbling block for me. And Rabbi Ann let me know that I could definitely move forward without learning to decode the Hebrew alphabet. My desire to learn more and grow spiritually was what counted. So here I am today.

Since in a traditional service, this is where the rabbi (or B'nei Mitzvah candidates) would give a D'var Torah, I am going to give a very brief one here. More, actually, a retelling of the book of Numbers as it relates to my personal journey.

This week's Parasha (Torah portion) is called "Sh'lach L'cha" (Numbers 13:1-15:41). In that portion, following G-d's instructions, Moses sends out a representative from each of the 12 tribes to scout out the land that G-d has promised to the Israelites. These are dark verses, full of drama and punishment, although the Promised Land is therein described as a land of "milk and honey." What interests me is discussing (very briefly, I promise) the book of Numbers itself. This is the fourth book of the Torah—which is made up of the five books in the Hebrew Bible. I am a book editor, and chronologically Numbers could have been the third book (rather than the fourth) because the period covered in Numbers begins about one year after the events in Exodus—which is the second book in the Torah, where the Israelites escape from Egypt, cross the Red Sea ("Sea of Reeds"), and arrive on the other side.

Numbers takes place during the approximately 40 years the Israelites wander in the desert (Sinai, the Negev, and Transjordan), and it ends just prior to their entering the Promised Land. This book is called Numbers (that's what we call it in English) because it lists a ton of numbers: lots of census records, the order of the 12 tribes and their marching hierarchy, and so on. Numbers has been called "The book of Israel's failings," but through those failings, the people learned and grew, and became a cohesive group. It took an entire generation for this to happen; most of the original people who had left Egypt grew old and died on their wanderings. A new generation was born in the desert (or had been youngsters when they left Egypt), and they grew to maturity and leadership during these 40 years. Many mistakes were made—which led to the development of laws. The religious hierarchy was established—which codified who would become the priests and clarified their powers (so tribal law, government, and religious hierarchy were established). We learn through our mistakes, and the Israelites became a nation during this challenging time of wandering in the desert and trying to live in such a way that G-d was commanding them to live.

I liken this primal journey to my own: a lot of wanderings and wrong turns, some extremely helpful for personal growth—others less so. When I was 13, the usual age for girls or boys to become Bat or Bar Mitzvah (a daughter or son of the commandment), girls were not yet given that opportunity in my community; although by the time my younger sister, Wendy, came of age, she did become a Bat Mitzvah. I was somewhere on the cusp, during a time when girls and women were not an integral part of the ritual fabric of Classical Reform Judaism. I wandered for many years, always feeling Jewish in my feminist heart, but not overtly so identified, especially with the male-centered practices of those times. I lived all over the world and was involved in many interesting situations (those adventures would be another whole long discussion). Eventually I returned home to New York, went to work with my mother, and met Larry.

So, my Jewish journey continues. I am on a path, still wandering, but this time it is a Jewish path. Jewish women (at least in Reform Judaism) began to reclaim and create spaces for ourselves at the center of Jewish life. We are no longer relegated to the outskirts of ritual but are rabbis and cantors and leaders in our communities. I feel a connection among the disparate parts of myself and am very excited about these developments. In fact, my dearest wish is to someday have the opportunity to take off enough time from work to be able to go to Israel to study Hebrew in an ulpan—a Hebrew language immersion program. That way I would come full circle: deepening my knowledge of Judaism and what it means to me as a Jewish woman, AND being able, finally, to decode that beautiful, musical, mysterious language.

I would like to thank my children for becoming my teachers. I want to thank my sister, Wendy, for traveling from North Carolina to cheer me on. I would like to thank the Temple Beth El board of directors for welcoming me as a board member and for supporting my endeavors. Many thanks to our temple Sisterhood for assisting with the luncheon downstairs; your help is very much appreciated. I want to thank Rabbi Ann for allowing me this opportunity and for all her encouragement; I will truly miss your monthly visits, although I know we will remain friends. And I want to thank Larry for his love these past 25 years.

David Kosins
Temple Beth Am (Seattle, Washington)

Several people, including my lovely wife of 24 years, have recently asked me why I decided I needed to have a second Bar Mitzvah, 40 years after my big fat Detroit extravaganza. After all, there are many ways I could have spent 60 or so Sunday mornings over the last two years besides learning my aleph-baiz and trying to keep pace with Rabbi Jonathan. Let me try to explain to you the reasons behind my *mishegas*.

A year ago, September, when I found out the others in my class had never had the opportunity to study for their B-Mitzvah, I went to Rabbi Jonathan and asked if it was okay for me to join them in their studies, since I had already become Bar Mitzvah once. He asked why I was interested and the first thing out of my mouth was, "This time I want to do it right." I went on to explain that back in 1969 I totally faked my way through my Haftarah by reading my transliteration when I should have been reading from the Hebrew. What kind of *mensch* gets away with that?

To me, the purpose of the Bar Mitzvah was to get enough gelt to pay for my dad to bring back a shiny new black Gibson Les Paul Custom from Manny's Music on one of his buying trips to New York. Remember, this was the year of Woodstock and no self-respecting guitar man would be caught dead playing the K-Mart special I purchased in the fourth grade. Hebrew school had been a nightmare for me. I remember freezing my *tukhis* off, standing outside McKinley Elementary, waiting for the yellow United Hebrew Congregation bus to schlep me to class, where I knew none of the kids, whose main objective was to terrorize the helpless teachers. My only memory, other than my frostbite, was how to say, "Be quiet!" in Hebrew. I endured this torture two or three days a week for a year or two before quitting. After this, my parents hired a *yeshiva bucher* with payes and B.O. to tutor me. Again, I learned nothing, and hated every minute. At age 12, I didn't have the foresight to connect my Hebrew lessons with the eventual electric guitar. My parents had *rachmones* (compassion) and fired the tutor. We got another. No different. I resisted learning and ditched my lessons whenever possible.

My family didn't belong to a synagogue even though my dad grew up in an Orthodox family from the old country and was in the *schmatte* business and we lived in a Jewish neighborhood. Dad's version of Judaism was: Work 90 hours a week so your family can have the possessions and opportunities not available to your immigrant parents. Mooch High Holiday tickets from a friend. Give tzedakah to the NAACP to support the *shvartzer* who buys your suits, washes your Cadillac, cleans your house. Say Kaddish when your parents die, *kine-ahora*. Belong to a Jewish country club. Tell your sons to be a doctor or a lawyer. Mom's version of Judaism was: G-d is everywhere so why do I need to go to shul? Have Nana and Papa over on Shabbes for a nice dinner with challah and candles. Make a lovely table for yontif, with wine and nut cake on Pesach. No need to bother with a Seder or blessings, but some "egg'n onion" matzah and Manischewitz are good. Light a menorah when the kids are little but do presents on Christmas day with the goyim. Only eat barbeque ribs or shrimp chow mein when you go out on Sunday nights. Serve *kichel* when the weekly mahjong ladies come over for a game. Send your kids to Jewish camps and your son to Hebrew school. Talk "Jewish" when you don't want the kinder to know the topic of conversation.

Since we never belonged to a shul, my only experience with rabbis was at funerals, weddings and Bar Mitzvahs. I'd been to a couple dozen of these, but they were either family affairs or a chance to enjoy another asthmatic hayride, make out with the latest Debbie, Suzie or Wendy, or groove to one of the Motor City's fine psychedelic bands. At my Bar Mitzvah, it was Mutzie and the Montegos.

So, when the time came for my one-on-one interview with the

Conservative rabbi who would be officiating, I was scared to death. I didn't know the rabbi or the other boy with whom I'd be sharing the bimah. I didn't know an Aleinu from an aliyah. I couldn't tell an ayin from a zayin. I failed all of the rabbi's questions. The one that was most humiliating was, "Name three famous American Jews." I assumed he meant notable scholars, philosophers, theologians, historians. I drew a blank. My mom was ashamed at my inability to respond. I think my dad was at work. Had I realized that any yid would do, I would have reeled off the Three Stooges, the Marx Brothers, Bob Dylan, Mike Bloomfield, Sandy Koufax, Leonard Bernstein, on and on. But instead, I wanted to run from the room and never come back. A memory almost as painful was walking alone to the neighborhood Conservative shul on Shabbes mornings to fulfill my obligation to attend services. I didn't know a soul, there were no kids, and I didn't understand a word of Hebrew. I was lonely, bored and resentful.

After writing my 300 thank-you notes and breaking in my new guitar, I dropped Judaism like a hot potato knish. It took Marvin Blake, my friend Jeff's dad, a prominent silver-tongued attorney, all of five minutes to persuade me to become an atheist. I left the suburban Detroit shtetl at my earliest opportunity and headed west. I wanted nothing to do with the clothing business and saw no percentage in tradition or ritual.

And yet, you can take the Jew out of the shtetl, but you can't take the shtetl out of the Jew. My cultural and ethnic and historical identity kept reasserting itself. Always inspired by Woody Allen, I wrote a 25-page research paper at U.C. Santa Cruz entitled *The Origin of Neurosis in American Jews*. I fell in love with a beautiful, brilliant Politics major from L.A. named Lois Soiffer. It was no accident she was Jewish; I had dreamt about California girls, but my subconscious steered me away from the shiksas. I chose a career that is as Jewish to my generation as being a tailor was to my Grandpa Max's generation. For graduate school projects, I recorded an oral history with my Yiddish-speaking Grandma Helen, and wrote an essay on Jewish death and mourning rituals. When Lois and I married, even though neither of us was from a strongly observant family, there was no question that we'd be wed under the chuppah. I hadn't been near a rabbi in 15 years and the only one we could relate to was Ted Falcon, because he was also a clinical psychologist. Shortly after our move to Seattle, Lois had to peel me out of the seat at the Guild 45th, 20 minutes after the conclusion of Schindler's List. I was sobbing uncontrollably, grieving for unnamed *mishpocheh* I never met.

We have always gravitated toward other tribesmen and women, and began to attend the occasional Seder, Hanukkah party, wedding, or bris. Fast forward to the birth of our daughter Rose in 1997. There was Rabbi Ted again for the baby naming. Having a Jewish baby reminded me that I'm Jewish too and that I have an obligation to teach her what I know. But I didn't know much. Rose took to Isaac Singer and Chelm Stories like a Jew to bagels. Progressing from Hadassah's Training Wheels to Kadima to Temple Beth Am, she has embraced her religious and cultural education, and inspired me to stay one step ahead of her. Klezmer music, European folktales, Shabbat dinners, my first Yom Kippur fast, the annual chicken soup-making marathon, and shvitzing with the boychiks led the way to Hebrew classes and eventually to the B-Mitzvah course.

Over time, I graduated from an atheist to an agnostic. I grew to value Jewish ritual, ethics, liturgical music, history and philosophy, not just corned beef and comedy. I even had fun learning the rudiments of the Hebrew language in a healing sort of way. Besides, it's good exercise for a middle-aged cerebral cortex. Using the Bar Mitzvah process to connect to my people across 6,000 years was the furthest thing from my mind when I was a little pisher in 1969. After years of alienation from my religion, I decided it was time to explore it in a deeper way that is meaningful for me, not just because it was expected by my parents. This time around, I wanted to "do it right." Your friendship and support have helped me achieve this goal. Thank you, and *Zei Gezunt*!

Rachel Moore
Temple Beth El (Tacoma, Washington)

My journey with Judaism has gone on all my life. While growing up in Auburn, Washington as a child, being Jewish always seemed to be the normal thing, and everyone else was just different—even though I was one of two Jewish kids in both my neighborhood and school. I thought it was great to be able to celebrate two New Years each year, have different foods at certain times of the year, learn a different language and history that the other kids didn't, and oddly enough I thought it was not only normal but cool to go to school six instead of five days a week. As I grew up, much like many people, I learned how being different, no matter how proud you are and want to share with others what makes yourself different, can reveal others' unacceptance. Others such as classmates, teachers, family members, and even co-workers who were non-Jews. While going through my teen and even my 20s trying to fit in with others to feel accepted and not be excluded without losing my Jewish identity was always a challenge. Whether it was with loss of a job due to another's prejudice or with dating where the other person would push their own beliefs onto me to try to change what I believe in because they don't agree. Especially when you are not connected and involved with your Jewish community.

Toward the end of my 20s, especially after some choices I made and people who crossed my path who only turned out to be toxic in my life, I focused on a positive path to being happy and healthy. That included going to a support group and counseling to help me work through some things I have gone through as well as get back to hobbies I've always enjoyed and people who are important to me before making the step to reconnect with Judaism and the community I grew up with. That is when I realized that has been the one thing I was missing for a long time. By reconnecting, I have been reminded of what I lost by being separate from community for so many years.

In the past year-and-a-half, I have worked hard to review, relearn, and gain clarification on the practices and history of Judaism, plus relearn Hebrew after not keeping up with it due to not having been involved with community to help reinforce things. As in this week's Torah reading which talks about being holy even while being different from others. In relearning and reconnecting with Judaism and this community, I feel I have also gained not only great friends and extended family, but also self-confidence, self-esteem, a better handle on personal insecurities, and the ability to accept myself fully even with friends who are non-Jews. I can be myself without worry of being ashamed of myself or become humiliated and embarrassed by others' unacceptance and judgements and still feel included among the Jewish community. No matter what phase of life I have gone through so far, being Jewish has always been and will continue being as much a part of what makes me the person I am as my red hair red and blue eyes. I am proud and grateful that my life has included Judaism. Being a part of it allows me to have a more enriched life than I would without it.

Terry Kraus
Congregation Emanu-El (San Francisco, California)

I entered the field of professional synagogue management in 1987. As a child, I had no synagogue affiliation; as a young married couple, we belonged to the synagogues where my husband tutored B-Mitzvah students. Although I felt competent in my jobs as executive director for the first 16 years of my career, and at Congregation Emanu-El in San Francisco as the director of membership services since 2003, I always felt something was missing, and I was envious of our young people who were learning so much.

In the fall of 2004, I took the leap and enrolled in the *Anshei Mitzvah* (adult Bar/Bat Mitzvah) class co-taught by Rabbi Helen Cohn and Cantor Roslyn Barak at Emanu-El. So many of us signed up that year that we met both as a full class of 16, and in our three separate groups as there were three ceremonies planned. Although nervous about the undertaking, my spring of 2005 trip to Israel with my colleagues through the National Association of Temple Administration reaffirmed that becoming an adult Bat Mitzvah was a good decision. Our group of five became Anshei Mitzvah in June of 2005, and I finally felt Jewishly empowered. I am grateful to my teachers and my fellow students for their support and I have used my experience to encourage others.

Elaine S. Lavine
East End Temple (New York, New York)

Although I (weirdly) enjoyed "Hebrew School" at a Conservative synagogue in upstate New York, I did not have a Bat Mitzvah ceremony. During most of my adulthood, I celebrated Jewish holidays, and would manage to attend High Holy Day services at one place or another, but I remained unaffiliated.

In 2005, my sister invited me to join her and her family on a trip to Israel. For 10 days we explored Israel from Eilat to Jerusalem. For the first time in my life, I was surrounded by Jews, in a Jewish country. Jews were old, Jews were young, Jews were religious, Jews were secular, and everything in between. Most especially, the Jews I met were fiercely proud, and Jewishly-engaged, however they each defined that.

When I returned home to New York City, wanting to make a public declaration about my Judaism, I was determined to find a synagogue, and learn to chant Torah. As I was walking around my neighborhood one day, I realized that there was a small Reform synagogue on a quiet street two blocks from my home: East End Temple. Completely new to a Friday night Reform service, I didn't know any of the melodies, not to mention the choreography. In fact, during my first L'cha Dodi, I faced the wrong direction, until someone gently corrected me.

After two or three weeks, I met with East End Temple's rabbi, and told him that I wanted to study a Torah portion, learn to chant it, and make this my Bat Mitzvah ceremony. Luckily, I had retained my ability to read Hebrew, so that eliminated one big hurdle. On a Friday night in November 2006, I successfully chanted a section of Torah, led the prayers, and delivered a D'var Torah. What I was also saying was, "I am Jewish, hear me roar!"

In the years since, I cemented my Jewish engagement as a volunteer and as an East End Temple board member, and continue to manage temple projects as a lay leader. Every year since that first time, I've chanted Torah two or three times during the year, including on Rosh Hashanah.

I've often told people that, starting with that first time in 2006, chanting Torah is my version of bungee-jumping. Each time I imagine everything going wrong, and I literally tremble with nervousness. Before I begin each time, my cantor reminds me to breathe. Then I chant the ancient words, finish, and can't wait to do it again. I am lucky and grateful that Torah is part of me, and I am part of this sacred whole.

Roberta Schiff
Congregation Shir Chadash (Freedom Plains, New York)

Become Bat Mitzvah at 13? At our Reform temple in Columbus, Ohio, this was not done. No one questioned it. There was a class leading to confirmation and I was part of that. But then we moved to California and did not join a congregation until it was time for my brother to become Bar Mitzvah. My Jewish education had ended. (I did write all his thank-you notes.)

I have belonged to several synagogues as an adult: in Los Angeles; Lawrence, Kansas; New York City; and since the early part of this century, to Congregation Shir Chadash in Freedom Plains, New York, near Poughkeepsie. I have always chosen smaller synagogues, as it is easier to make friends and form community. Also, one knows that whatever one has to offer it is imperative to get involved as no one else may provide that service. I love our husband and wife duo, Rabbi Daniel Polish and Cantor Gail Hirschenfang, our evolving liturgy and rituals, and the service we provide to both our synagogue community and our social action outreach to the larger community. All this is very meaningful to me, but I also identify very strongly as a vegan and feel that this aligns very closely with Jewish values. Although most people really enjoy the food I bring, and some say I have made a difference, there is no one in the congregation who has come forth to join me. I experience the duality of being both an active member and an outsider.

Why did I join the adult B-Mitzvah class? Because the cantor asked me to come to the introductory meeting. As our grandparents would have said—"Vell, it couldn't hoit, just go." So, I went and there was an almost instant bonding among us and the cantor. I joined; we prepared for 18 months. Coming together once a week to study together is joyful, life-enhancing and challenging. Jews are taught to honor our parents, visit the sick, celebrate with the bride and groom, but this directive ends with the admonition that the study of Torah outweighs all other commandments. So, I went each Tuesday evening, sometimes well prepared and sometime not so much. I felt good when I could keep up and played the "old lady" card when I did not meet my expectations. I turned 80 six months before our big day while my six classmates approached or slightly passed the half-century mark.

On 24 Iyyar 5777 (May 20, 2017) we led the service, chanted our parasha and gave our talk on B'har. We felt fulfilled and our families, friends and congregants shared in our accomplishment. We continue to study and will read Genesis on Simchat Torah.

I am pleased to be able to both read Torah and bake and bring vegan challah.

With love and appreciation to our Cantor and my six B-Mitzvah sisters.

Rocille McConnell
Congregation Emanu-El B'ne Jeshurun
(Milwaukee, Wisconsin)

I have been a Jew all my life. My family attended the Reform temple in St. Paul, Minnesota. My home was not traditional in that there was no Shabbat celebration each Friday. We went to services very little (except for the High Holidays) and celebrated Pesach at my grandparents' homes. I did attend Sunday school, was confirmed (that was the term used in the past), and like most girls, did not attend Hebrew school. Bat Mitzvah was unheard of in that era.

Going to a Jewish camp for three of my teen years had a big influence on me. I digested all that was Jewish, and that I had not been exposed to. I even came home and asked if we could keep kosher. The response was, "You can do that when you have your own home."

My first marriage was to a conservative Jew. So, I was delighted to now practice all the aspects of Jewish life in the home and synagogue that I had missed up to this point. My second marriage was to a Jew by choice. He also found joy and satisfaction in a Jewish home, holidays, and being active in the synagogue.

Toward the end of his life, we desired to explore Reconstruction Judaism and found this type still maintained the principles of the service but with more creativity. The congregants also exuded warmth and compassion that was so welcoming.

Two years ago, I felt a need to attend services on a weekly basis, not just twice a month, and be more stimulated by study. I desired a temple which would feel more like my second home. CEEBJ was definitely the right move.

Besides attending weekly Friday night services or Saturday morning minyan, I desired to participate in the myriad activities and social justice opportunities that were offered. And of course, I was especially excited about the Anshe Mitzvah program: two years of commitment every Tuesday evening studying with our rabbis and cantor. I have always maintained that learning is a lifelong process, and this course certainly proved that point.

Anshe Mitzvah has assisted me in seeking answers to unresolved personal questions that have evolved during my lifetime. It has also widened my faith's horizons including the Jewish circle of life, the aspects of prayer, past and present Reform Judaism. I started learning to read Hebrew innumerable times and then stopped using it. With Anshe Mitzvah, I received the most thorough study of the language, and I am committed to continue using it during services and opportunities to read Torah.

I am truly awed to be standing on this bimah participating in this special Shabbat service with my five classmates. I want to express deep gratitude to you: Rabbi Berkson, Rabbi Barlosky, and Cantor Barash for imparting your knowledge to me on a wide range of Jewish topics, a love for the Hebrew language, to chant the Holy Scriptures. . . and most important, to be proud of my Jewish heritage.

Loretta Shapiro
Hebrew Benevolent Congregation – "The Temple"
(Atlanta, Georgia)

I grew up in rural Georgia in a small town with two Jewish families. I never attended Sunday/Hebrew school and rarely went to a synagogue service. I met my husband at the University of Georgia. Soon after that we moved to Atlanta. Over the course of time we moved from Orthodox to Conservative to Reform congregations.

After joining The Temple (Hebrew Benevolent Congregation), I enrolled in the adult B'nei Mitzvah class taught by Rabbi Steven Rau and Cantor Deborah Hartman. I learned to read Hebrew and chant Torah. What an experience! I found such a meaningful way to express my love of my Jewish faith and my devotion to all my family who came before me. When I chant from the Torah scroll, I feel a direct connection to them.

My grandfather of blessed memory always wanted me to be President of the United States. I'm sure he never thought there was any way I could become Bat Mitzvah. I'm sorry he did not live to see it. It would have made him prouder than being grandfather of the president.

I now tutor Bar and Bat Mitzvah students at The Temple. It is a sweet and rewarding experience for me to play a part in passing on the rich heritage of our people to another generation and to watch them take their place in an unbroken chain from Sinai to the present and into the future. It is a blessing.

Francie Schwarz
Hebrew Benevolent Congregation – "The Temple"
(Atlanta, Georgia)

Three years ago, I became a Bat Mitzvah as part of the adult B'nei Mitzvah class at The Temple. Below is a quick summary of what inspired me to do so.

I grew up in Montgomery, Alabama where we had a small but close Jewish community. Surprisingly, we had three synagogues: Conservative, Reform and Sephardic. I was a member of the Reform synagogue where the tradition of Bat and Bar Mitzvah was not observed. I had a close relationship with my rabbi, Rabbi Peter Baylinson, which only grew closer after my mother died at the early age of 48 when I was 11 years old. Although I always connected with being Jewish, I never really understood nor desired to have a stronger Jewish identity. My father was a very intellectual Jew but for some reason we celebrated Christmas throughout the years of my childhood.

So, what inspired me?

I have two daughters who are 17 months apart, so we decided to have their Bat Mitzvah ceremonies together in Israel with their two cousins. As an adult, I had often thought about studying to become a Bat Mitzvah; but now I knew it was something I had to experience along with my two girls. I was 50 years old—two years older than my Mother when she died—and it was a time of reflection for me. I had a high-power job that began to define me, and I realized I needed something to ground me and connect me to something with much greater meaning.

My adult Bat Mitzvah experience was amazing. My daughters were as proud of me as I was of them (it's not easy to teach an old dog new tricks), and we as a family had a year of Bat Mitzvah celebrations: me with my class in early May; the girls with their cousins in Israel in June; and a family B-Mitzvah where Marissa, Genna, and I read from the Torah and celebrated with family and friends. It was the year of the Bat Mitzvah and a year I will never forget.

Fred Schwartz
Portland, Oregon

My name is Esther Schwartz. My husband, Fred, became a Bar
Mitzvah along with three amazing women in our congregation in
May of 2017. He was 84 at the time. He did a great job and his
family and friends were so proud of him and admired his accomplishment so much. It's a bittersweet story, as Fred died on July
27, 2017. He had been ill for most of 2017, but that did not keep
him from his studies for his Bar Mitzvah. His classmates and our
wonderful rabbi were also immensely helpful, supportive, and encouraging.

Fred's D'var Torah for Parasha K'doshim
"And G-d spoke to Moshe saying, 'Speak to the entire Community of Israel, and say to them: you shall be holy, for I, the Lord,
your G-d, am holy.'" This Torah portion outlines man's laws gov-
erning man's relationship with his fellow man. Despite the ethical
emphasis of many of the commandments, this section also deals
with ritual concerns. What is most striking is the intertwining of
laws that are man-oriented with commandments which are G-d-
oriented.

Ramban explains that one can keep kosher but still eat like a
pig. The concept here is that keeping to the letter of the law is
not enough. The law is to keep the laws of kashrut; but we must
go beyond that standard. Applying "you shall BE holy" implies
another layer of sensitivity and mindfulness that we must bring to
the commandment.

We are also commanded that when we reap our harvest, we must
leave the edges for the poor and the stranger. The law says, "You
shall not pick your vineyard bare." This goes far beyond not breaking the specific law. It is much more than just going through the
motions of carrying out the law. It is also concern and care for

those less fortunate.

So, who is holy? How is it possible for man to be holy? Kol Adat B'nai Yisrael; it is "the entire Israelite community" which is holy. Holiness is commanded of everyone. When G-d instructed Moses to call all the people together to give them the commandment to BE holy, it was so that it would be clear to all that holiness is not something achievable by only the few, the high and mighty, the rich; but by all.

So, while the Torah provides us guidance for proper behavior toward our fellow man, it also leaves us with a question. To act or not to act. If the law does not educate us sufficiently to behave properly, what does? How can one be a good person and live a holy life? That is the question we must ponder in each situation as we live our lives.

The standard is more than being observant and following the law. Generosity, helpfulness, honesty and kindness all matter when we, as individuals, interact with another.

You might be wondering what motivated me to become a Bar Mitzvah so late in life. It is something I have thought about for quite some time, and decided if not now, when? Judaism has come to play a more central role in my life now than it did when I was a younger man. To become a Bar Mitzvah seemed like a natural choice. I know I made the right decision.

I want to take this opportunity to add my deepest thanks to my wonderful wife, Esther; my children, Todd and Gail; my daughter-in-law, Linda; and my grandchildren, Moriah, Joshua and Kaylen, who have been the greatest blessings of my life. Their love, support and encouragement have been constant. I want to also thank all my friends, Rabbi Berg, and my three wonderful classmates for all they have taught me, for sharing this journey with me and for their many kindnesses.

Joyce Solochek
Congregation Emanu El B'nai Jeshurun
(Milwaukee, Wisconsin)

I have lived a wonderful, full Jewish life. Albert and I taught religious school the entire time our children were in school, as did my mother before us, because we felt it was important to show our girls how important a Jewish education was. On Friday nights we celebrate Shabbat dinner with our family, which I'm afraid now only includes the dog; but Felicia and Elizabeth seldom miss the unforgettable extended family gatherings for all the holidays, even though they now live far away.

Something has been missing in my Jewish life, however. Here I am this lifelong Women's Libber, as evidenced by my career as a chemist, but I bought into the prevailing point of view when I was a teen that only boys learned Hebrew. I came to all the services at the synagogue and sat there like a dummy, or read the transliteration, which meant absolutely nothing to me. As I got older I questioned how could I consider myself a full participant? I felt that I needed to learn to read Hebrew and to chant Torah and Haftorah. Therefore, the first thing I did when I retired was sign up for Anshe Mitzvah.

This has been a very rewarding two years. I discovered that my task was much more difficult than I had expected, and I now more fully appreciate how remarkable my daughters were at their B'not Mitzvah. I enjoy being a member of the congregation so much more, now that I can read along, although slowly, and can recognize the trope when someone is reading from the Torah. Anshe Mitzvah has allowed me to round out my life as a Jew. I also feel more a part of the Emanu El community because of the two years of shared experiences with my Anshe Mitzvah friends, and the knowledge and friendship from Rabbis Berkson and Barlosky, and from Cantor Barash, along with his kindness and extreme patience.

The one nice thing about waiting until now instead of becoming Bat Mitzvah at 13 is that not only do I get to share this special moment with my family, but, as a bonus, with my wonderful grandchildren Sophie, Lilah, Jake and Sydney. You guys are next.

Barbara Feller
Temple Judah (Cedar Rapids, Iowa)

My older daughter, Heidi, turned 12 on April 11, 1992. She became a Bat Mitzvah on that very same day. My mother, who was born on April 7, 1924, had always joked that she and Heidi shared a birth month and must, therefore, be of similar age. So, when Heidi started preparing for her all-important date, her grandmother became her partner and ceremoniously entered the world of Jewish adulthood at the age of 68.

At Temple Judah in Cedar Rapids, Iowa, besides being called to read from Torah, the Bar or Bat Mitzvah leads the entire service on both Friday night and Saturday morning. This takes a minimum of a year of study. Both my mother and daughter worked extremely hard in their preparations.

In addition, our tradition is that on Saturday morning, the Torah is literally handed from generation to generation as the family stands on the bimah and hands it from grandparents to parents to the student. I wasn't sure how this would be handled for our situation. Besides the double generation, I was concerned because when I attended Hebrew school as a child, in Gloversville, New York, I had been told I could never even touch a Torah since I was female. Of course, this meant I had never become a Bat Mitzvah.

I went to Rabbi Chesman for advice. He told me not to worry. He said that when the time came, he would call me up with my younger daughter, Rachel (Ray). I felt this made sense and was happy with his answer.

As you might imagine, the whole event was a very special moment for our entire family. Since Passover was fast approaching, Heidi wrote a speech which told the story of how the "knight" by her side was different from all others. My mom's speech told of becoming a fountain pen, the signature gift for a Bar Mitzvah in her day. My dad, my brother, my husband, Ray and I all shared in the writing of a special message of pride for the accomplishments both Heidi and Mom so well deserved.

I wrote this emotional speech on our family's new contraption, a home computer. In those days, the sheets of paper were attached and fed through the printer by a series of holes punched along the edges. I jokingly left these sheets in a long stream which I waved in front of our congregation when it came time for my presentation. I am sure there wasn't a dry eye in the place.

But it wasn't even close to over yet.

When Rabbi Chesman stood to make his comments, I was shocked to hear an announcement that the congregation were all invited to part II of this multi-generational event when Rachel and I would be called to the Torah in 1994!

I learned that when the rabbi told me I'd be called up with my younger daughter, he meant I was being invited to become a Bat Mitzvah too. I was frightened by this and was not shy about telling him so. He said not to worry, as no one would remember anyway. Rabbi Chesman was a very wise man. I'm sure he knew, even as he spoke, that no one was going to forget. Least of all...me!

On February 18, 1994, Rachel Shimona Feller and her mom, Barbara Feller, shared a B-Mitzvah of their own. I had sat through classes of Hebrew and trope, learned the Sephardic pronunciations of vowels and letters and became a more dedicated member of my community. Ray and I held hands during the entire service. To this day I feel a wave of relief and exaltation whenever I hear the chanting of the ending prayer of Haftorah.

I cannot begin to describe the emotional fulfillment these events had for all of us.

When my mom passed away in 1997, she was buried in the dress she wore when she became an adult.

Unfortunately, our Rabbi Chesman was taken all too soon as well. But even in some of his last conversations, he'd make mention of those times. And when he did so, tears would mist his eyes.

As it happens, I now teach beginning Hebrew to students at Temple Judah. I feel that I have a real empathy for what they are doing...and we all have a great deal of fun together.

I will turn 68 at my next birthday. This is the same age as my mom became an adult. I suppose I am now one as well.

Jessica Donath
Congregation Beth Chayim Chadashim
(Los Angeles, California)

A Sense of Religious Normalcy

For much of my adult life, I left the "religion" line blank on various forms I had to fill out. What was I supposed to write? I never had a christening or baptism, nor a confirmation, baby naming or Bat Mitzvah.

My otherwise wonderful parents decided to leave my religious identity up to me. They expected things would fall all into place like magic and my true spiritual being would reveal itself when I was old enough.

I don't blame them. In 1978, when I was born, they didn't want an argument over religion to taint a time full of excitement and anticipation.

In the past, they had argued enough—about my dad being six years younger than my mom and not ready (read: *fit*) to start a family; about the fact that neither of them had family around to help with a baby; and about history.

When my mom married my dad, she told him she wasn't going to give up her Christianity. He said, "fine." When his Holocaust survivor parents said they could only accept a German shiksah in the family if potential children would at least be introduced to Judaism, my mom said, "fine."

And since my secular father didn't make any effort to keep his commitment to his parents, my mom took it upon herself to read books and teach me what she had learned.

So, I lived a happily secular interfaith life. I opted out of Christian religion lessons in high school so I could sleep in twice a week. Instead, I went to the Jewish community center in Frankfurt to learn about Jewish holidays with my cousins.

In elementary school, I brought the matzah when our protestant religion teacher wanted to teach the class about Pesach and Easter.

I was the only student who cried during a Holocaust documentary; and I took advantage of my German teacher who had significant guilt issues. She gave me better grades because, "Jews are such wonderful people. Isn't your dad Jewish?"

But becoming Bat Mitzvah wasn't an option.

Even though German Jews invented Reform Judaism in the early nineteenth century, it wasn't a thing when I grew up in the 80s and 90s.

After WWII, when only a few Jews remained or returned, German Jewry came up with the concept of "Einheitsgemeinde," unity congregation. The leadership (both clergy and administrative) would be Orthodox, but Jews of different backgrounds would be welcomed.

For someone like me, that didn't work. Girls could not become Bat Mitzvah—especially not one with a Christian mother who refused to take part in any kind of conversion.

But since I was never masochistic enough to desire the approval of a people or groups who rejected me or discriminated against me, I didn't really care. I never blamed Judaism for the hostility I felt directed toward me. I always thought people interpreted scripture in a way that helped them feel better about themselves.

As far as I was concerned, I was just as Jewish as my cousins.

Even when I moved to the U.S. in 2009, becoming Bat Mitzvah was the farthest thing from my mind. I wanted to be with my boyfriend of a year.

I wanted to buy our first piece of furniture together. We still own the brown day bed from Crate and Barrel that nearly ended our relationship and put me on the next flight back to Germany.

To say Germany was a majority Christian country would be like saying that the NFL has a lot of African American players. Stores are closed on Sundays and Germans get at least one long weekend each month caused by some (often minor) religious holiday.

Los Angeles is different. I was shocked to find such a vibrant and diverse Jewish life. And so many kosher food options! The kosher store in Frankfurt only opened a couple of hours each Friday so people could buy what they needed for Shabbat.

I began to study journalism at the University of Southern California. For one of my classes, I had to report on American Jews. At the same time, I enrolled in a course that would take me to the beit din (religious court) to confirm my status according to Jewish law.

I prefer "confirm" instead of "convert" because I never had any other religion that I left behind when I joined the tribe.

Doing research for this story about American Jews, I stumbled across congregation Beth Chayim Chadashim (BCC) in Los Angeles. It's the first Jewish congregation founded by and for gay and lesbian Jews. That is its claim to fame in a city that is home to Kirk Douglas' shul as well as Michael Jackson's Jewish guru.

I had no idea that gay Jews existed. And if they had their own congregation, they must have enough for a minyan.

When I interviewed BCC's Rabbi Lisa Edwards for a Valentine's Day story about gay marriage, I fell in love. I asked her to be my sponsoring rabbi for my confirmation. She agreed.

Right away I knew I wanted to join when some congregants discussed wanting to start a study group of adults who wanted to become B-Mitzvah. My son was only a few months old when the weekly classes began.

I don't remember my Torah portion, but I do remember giving a little drash about my son based on the haftorah portion. Something about kids cutting their teeth on parents and me cutting my teeth on G-d.

In a way, reading from the Torah in front of G-d, my new spiritual home, as well as my family and friends, meant more for my arrival as a full and equal member of the Jewish faith than going to the beit din.

It gave me a sense of religious normalcy. In the U.S., most boys and girls can become Bar or Bat Mitzvah. My congregation gave me the opportunity to maintain the correct order of history, in the sense that I had my ceremony before my son will have his.

Going to the beit din felt good, but I wanted those signatures on the form mostly to spite others. The ones who had doubted my Jewishness and those who said I didn't belong because I didn't have a Jewish mother; that I wasn't equal.

That's done. By becoming Bat Mitzvah at the age of 35 I demonstrated to myself (and others) that I do belong—and have always belonged; and that I am equal.

Perhaps my parents were right after all. My religious identity did reveal itself when I was ready. It just took a little longer than expected.

Nina Bernstein
Temple Beth Hillel (Valley Village, California)

When our daughter turned five, we joined Temple Beth Hillel. We wanted her to learn about her heritage, what it was like to be a Jew. At the same time, I felt I was unable to help explain traditions and holidays, and knew I needed, and wanted, to learn more. I had grown up in a Jewish family to be sure, but aside from learning which food to serve when, there was very little else.

My husband had been brought up in a Conservative household, but had lived for a long time not being observant. High holidays, no; Christmas trees, yes. So, it was up to me.

At first, I joined a class about Jewish traditions taught by Patti Golden. It was wonderful to be able to actually learn what each holiday meant—more than just a meal! It was good but not enough.

I decided to become a Bat Mitzvah in the early 1980s, well before my daughter would be a Bat Mitzvah. It wasn't easy—going to classes, learning history, learning to read Hebrew—but I stuck to it. I don't remember much about the classes, but it must have made an impression as today I can still read along in the siddur and I celebrate the holidays; but more importantly, I never doubt my heritage.

Years later I created a group for younger women in the temple, called I'sha L'isha. In this study group, women wrapped tefillin, held a Torah and yad (many for the first time), and delved deeper into Jewish women's lives.

We recently moved to Northern California, and so many papers were tossed or got lost in the shuffle. However, I did find a poem that I had written for my Bat Mitzvah. The day included every class member writing about their experience. I remember writing it, as well as reading from the bimah.

Sunday mornings once so lazy
Now are rushed and filled with din.

Up late last night—my mind still hazy,
Open mouth and shove toast in.

Religious school at half past nine
Should give me just a little space.
But no—there's another class that's mine.
It starts at nine—step up the pace!

I like to get my daughter going.
Start her dressing, make her food.
Her father can finish—hear the groaning.
They're both still sleeping, in a terrible mood.
I've left myself a quarter hour.
Get myself dressed and the rest.
Those two are still looking quite sour.
Well, at least I've done my best.

Grab my books, give her some money.
I'm on my way, it isn't far.
Sorry Sunday morning's crazy honey.
Thoughts come together in the car.

I've made the class with time to spare.
First some coffee, then begin.
He wants me to read the Hebrew where?
Is my Hebrew name Muriel or Miriam?

Torah portions, try to read.
Any questions, let him know.
An extra year is what I need.
Such a short time in this year to go.

Next class starts right after this.

Our teacher is the Rabbi Jim.
I'll learn to be a basic Jewess.
It starts you stirring from within.

Is it worth the effort, time?
Will I be a better Jew?
Will I sit in temple and feel sublime?
To have facts about where, why or who?

I completed the class, the year's at an end
And today I can truly confess.
If I were given the choice to do it again
If even more obstacles were thrown in and then
If I thought it would end just the way this will end
My answer—most definitely. Yes!

Judy Zimmerman
Temple Beth Elohim (Wellesley, Massachusetts)

I grew up Reform in the Midwest. Being Jewish for me was more cultural than educational. It was about family and traditions, of which I have very fond memories, and I have relied upon in raising my own family. But, I'm embarrassed to say that I didn't even know the Shehecheyanu until my daughter's baby naming, when I was 30 years old. It wasn't until my kids entered the preschool at our temple, Temple Beth Elohim in Wellesley, Massachusetts, that I really started learning more about Judaism. As my husband and I were beginning to raise our own family, I knew then that it was important for me to understand more than just how to bake my mom's famous strudel for the High Holy Days.

When my oldest child started preparing to become a Bat Mitzvah, it was then I began thinking about the possibility that I would someday become Bat Mitzvah as an adult. After all, three of my children became Bat/Bar Mitzvah; it was time for me to focus on my direction and goals.

At age 50, I decided to join the temple's adult B-Mitzvah class. I am an active member at my temple, and I decided that this was the next step in my Jewish journey. I am very proud that I followed through with the challenge of learning Hebrew, and the feeling that day chanting from the Torah on the bimah in front of my friends and family was more emotional than I could have imagined. However, the experience of becoming a Bat Mitzvah as an adult also directed me to reflect on how I live my life through a Jewish lens, and delve deeper into learning and connecting with my community at Temple Beth Elohim, bringing me back to the sacred space and helping me to redefine my own Jewish identity.

Jodie LeVitus-Francisco
University Synagogue (Los Angeles, California)

I would like to start by thanking Cantor Jay, Rabbi Feinstein and Hal Daum for all of their help in getting me here, thank you all so much! I would also like to thank Dana and Joyce for their patience, help and support. Finally, I would like to thank my family, friends and husband Steve for encouraging me, supporting me and being here with me tonight. It really means a lot!

This is my story:

I was brought up in a Reform temple in Chicago, until my mom remarried when I was 10. My stepdad came from a very Conservative, almost Orthodox background. I dropped out of Hebrew school when I was about 11. I remember going to my brother's Bar Mitzvah, and he didn't know his haftorah, and I thought I didn't want to get up in front of all my family and friends and not be prepared. My sister recently told me she remembers me sitting on our couch saying I hate Hebrew school; I don't want to go. I don't really remember that part, but I do remember saying that I didn't want to continue. I think that because my mom had recently remarried, this was a battle she didn't want to get into with me, so she let me drop out. And so today, it is I who have chosen to study Hebrew, on my own, with no parents around to push me, or unfortunately be here with me to witness my progress. But it is because of this that it makes it that much more meaningful to me. I chose to learn this on my own in my own time, and I will always be grateful to my mom and my stepdad for allowing me to make that choice. I only wish that they could be with me here today to watch me as I become a Bat Mitzvah.

To me, part of the Jewish experience was celebrating all of the holidays with extended family, and in Chicago, the extended family was very large! Since coming to California in 1978, I haven't had family here to celebrate any of the holidays, and it has been very hard. I would try to find a temple or a service to go to for the high holidays, and my mom always encouraged me to go, to meet other Jewish people. It turns out that most of the services that I would go to turned out to be Orthodox services, and coming from a much more Reform background, I didn't feel connected in any way.

As I've gotten older, I find myself wanting to go to High Holiday services—especially for Yizkor, so that I can honor my mother. This past year at Rosh Hashanah, my fellow classmate Dana and I were walking back to her house, and I told her that I always thought about going back to learn Hebrew and become Bat Mitzvah. Ironically, she told me she wanted to do the same thing. We called University Synagogue and found out they had a program starting right away. Better yet, I had a connection to the temple as Rabbi Freehling had married my husband and me 13 years ago. My goal in doing this has been to be able to participate more in services and holidays; but my biggest goal is to be able to recite the mourner's Kaddish to honor my mother. When we started, I couldn't even follow along with the transliteration; and now, here I am reading Hebrew from the Torah! If my mother were alive today, I know she would be very proud of me, and I know in my heart that she is here with me today, as I stand before you on the bimah. I dedicate this honor of becoming a Bat Mitzvah to the memory of my mother, Joan Lee Kreiter.

Lynn Sheeran
Temple Beth El (Bloomfield Township, Michigan)

The portion I read describes G-d's instruction to Moses that he speak to the Israelite people and tell them to make fringes on the corners of their tallit and attach a cord of blue at each corner. This was so that the Jewish people would look at the fringes and remember the commandments and our covenant with G-d.

I proudly stand before the congregation, wearing MY tallit for the first time. For me, it is a symbol that connects me to my Jewish community and reminds me, in particular, of my Zayda. When I was a young girl, we would go to synagogue together and I remember him saying a prayer and putting on his tallit. As he followed along with the service, he would chant the Hebrew while I would read the English translation. When I was with my Zayda, I always felt so loved, safe, and warm. I feel the same way wearing my own tallit—as though my Zayda, now long gone, is still right there with me—giving me one of his great, warm hugs. I know both he and my beloved mother were with me that day in spirit and are proud of the journey I have taken that has led me to that moment; a 50-year-old dream finally realized … to become Bat Mitzvah. And yes, I'm proud of me too!

***

As I stood before this congregation, I recalled the first time ever attending a service there only two short years ago. New to Michigan, I felt nervous and out of place. But instead, the members of that community welcomed me with kind words and open arms. And while some of them may not know this, another dream of mine has been realized—to join a synagogue and experience that feeling of belonging. Temple Beth El became like a second home to me and for that, I am truly grateful.

In the past, I had always identified as more "culturally" Jewish. Now, more than ever, I feel closely connected to the rituals and words of our faith. Until that moment, I had been Jewish and had been a woman. This ceremony melded the two together and I am finally whole.

David L. Motz
Temple Beth Hillel (Valley Village, California)

SHALOM. On June 4th, 1983, a small B-Mitzvah group from Temple Beth Hillel was called to the Torah. As a member of that group, this essay partially explains why I chose to become Bar Mitzvah as an adult. As Jews very well over the age of 13, we were all already adults in the eyes of the Jewish community. So, this B-Mitzvah did not just mark our coming of age; rather, there must have been some other reason why we chose to do this.

My Bar Mitzvah story begins in childhood. I grew up in Long Beach, California in a white lower middle class non-Jewish community. I am an only child. My friends were non-Jewish. My school was non-Jewish. We didn't belong to a temple. I had no formal Jewish education. In short, the vast majority of my experiences were non-Jewish. Notice I don't say Christian. There is a difference between non-Jewish and Christian. What I learned of Judaism I learned in the home. I learned that we didn't believe in Jesus. I learned that we celebrated Hanukkah instead of Christmas. I learned about the Holocaust. I learned that there were people who persecuted Jews. There was a lot of love in my home. There was a lot of laughter. I had no doubt that my parents loved me. I had a healthy happy childhood. And I thank my parents for what they gave me.

My Jewish experiences were more in response to the non-Jewish world that surrounded me than positive affirmation of my heritage. For example, at my school we had a Christmas show—not a holiday show—a Christmas show. We would file into the auditorium. It would be decorated in red and green and gold tinsel. Someone would come out from behind the curtain and tell us the story of the three wise men. There would be Christmas carols from many lands and a Hanukkah song or two amidst it all. It was easy to get the impression that Hanukkah was just a unique way of celebrating

Christmas.
Let me give you the version of the Hanukkah song I learned...

Oh, Hanukkah, Oh, Hanukkah
Come light the menorah
Let's have a party
We'll all dance the hora
Gather round the table, we'll give you a treat
Sevivonim to play with and latkes to eat

And while we are playing
The candles are burning low
One for each night, they shed a sweet light
To remind us of days long ago
One for each night, they shed a sweet light
To remind us of days long ago...

O Star of wonder, star of night
Star with royal beauty bright
Westward leading, still proceeding
Guide us to thy Perfect Light.

Did anyone ever burn any crosses on our front lawn? No. Did anyone ever chase me home from school? Or call me names? No. But at the same time, I grew up in a culture that I knew I didn't belong to. I'm not unique in this regard. Jews are after all a minority in the U.S. But where I do feel unique is in a lack of positive Jewish experiences to balance out the influences of my non-Jewish community.

I did have Jewish role models. I'm sure every Jewish boy learned that Sandy Koufax is Jewish. And this is very interesting. I remember having various TV or film stars pointed out to me as being Jewish. They didn't stand up on the stage wearing a yarmulke and say, "I'm Jewish." But it would be tacitly known, somehow, that they were Jewish.

There's a flip side to this. I remember when we heard that President Kennedy had been assassinated. I remember my mother saying, "I hope Oswald isn't Jewish." Why would she say such a thing? It was because the memories of anti-Semitism were very fresh for my mother. Yes, as a Jew I was different.

So, let me ask you a question. What kind of sandwich can you make with matzo? Peanut butter and jam sandwiches, of course. And so, for the week of Passover I took peanut butter and jam sandwiches to school. And this was one of the few times that my friends realized that I was different—that I was Jewish. I knew the story of Passover. I'm not sure how. It must have been from home. And there was the movie *The Ten Commandments*. Growing up in the 50s and 60s also meant growing up with television. Let me share a story with you that helps to explain my desire to be here now.

I remember watching a television program called *Sam Benedict*. It starred Edmond O'Brien as a San Francisco attorney. Sam Benedict was based on real-life lawyer Jacob W. "Jake" Ehrlich. He was always very busy handling cases for clients who could never pay him. And I remember a particular episode when he was approached by a friend to be part of a minyan. It was Sam's job to run around town and find 8 or 9 Jewish men who had become Bar Mitzvah to be part of this minyan. In the time period portrayed, women need not have applied. And Sam went to the baker and the owner of the delicatessen. And there were other story lines which aren't important. But anyway, he got them all together for whatever the event was. And I remember sitting there and watching this and feeling very sad. Why? Because I thought that I couldn't have participated because I had not become Bar Mitzvah. And it's this feeling of wanting to belong, officially in some sense, which brings me to this moment. There are many of you who may have difficulty understanding how hard it is to be a Jew without knowledge of the religion and history, which makes you comfortable with your Judaism. My wife, for example, grew up as a temple member and Barbara went to a predominantly Jewish high school—Hamilton High.

And it is my wife's family that is in a large part responsible for my becoming Bar Mitzvah, although I'm sure they never realized it. The warmth (and sometimes heat) of their family dinners with blessings over the wine and bread... Attending High Holy Day services... Discussing sermons, not always agreeing, but discussing... These gave me positive Jewish experiences and made me want to participate, as they do, in the Jewish community; and made me want to learn more. I'm sure they never realized what I was thinking. To them I already belonged, they loved me...

I began this essay with Shalom. It's a word meaning, of course, peace. But it's a word having many other meanings for me. It was the first Hebrew word that our B–Mitzvah teacher taught us to read. Shalom is from the Hebrew root meaning completeness, wholeness, integrity. This is what I'm trying to achieve in my Jewish identity. It is also the word of greeting that one hears when one calls the temple. And this used to be quite unsettling to me. For I would be in some non-Jewish environment and I would phone the temple and the person would say, "Shalom" and I would be surprised and suddenly reminded that I was Jewish. I would be unsettled. I'm no longer unsettled in my Judaism. Shalom.

DeeGee Liniado
Congregation Gates of Prayer (Metairie, Louisiana)

I didn't set out to become Bat Mitzvah. Many years ago, when my children were young (the "baby" is almost 27), I started adult Hebrew a few different times. But, whether it was a sick child, a school program, or cancelled babysitter, I couldn't make it to classes regularly enough, and I dropped out.

In the decades since, I became a more active Sisterhood member (even serving as president) and congregant. I enjoyed singing the many prayers and blessings that are a part of our services, but I relied on transliteration and was no longer content with that.

When adult Hebrew was being offered again three years ago, a couple of my mah-jongg sisters and I decided to sign up together. If I would mention to someone that I was taking Hebrew, the frequent reaction was, "Oh, you're going to have a Bat Mitzvah?" My response, at least during the first year, was, "Not necessarily. I'm learning to be able to follow and more fully participate in services. I'll see how it goes."

While the class started with about seven students, after the first few months, many fell by the wayside just as I had on my previous attempts. The three of us were the last ones standing. And, with there being strength in numbers, we depended on each other, supported one another, and—most importantly for me—held each other accountable for showing up. Going out for dinner together after class was a fun reward.

As we neared the end of year one, I had to decide whether or not I was going to move forward with adult Bat Mitzvah as the destination. We three began discussing how we might go about it and, due at least in part to the fact that we have many friends in common, the idea of a fun Saturday night party to celebrate our accomplishment began to take shape. We went into the summer hiatus with our assignments of who would lead which parts of the service.

Even though formal classes weren't held during those months, the three of us continued to meet and practice.

The most difficult part of the process? Selecting a date. With Jazz Fest, Tulane graduation (attendance required for one of us), the synagogue gala, and a 13-year-old's Bar Mitzvah (imagine!) taking up many of the spring weekends, we were left with one option. And that Torah portion? What else but Metzorah—leprosy! Despite our initial disappointment with the subject matter, we each found a part that spoke to us and delivered a very personal D'var Torah.

Just like the typical Bat Mitzvah, we worried over what we would wear, and being nervous about making a mistake. Unlike the 13-year-olds, we didn't have braces, homework or exams, but we were making all our own arrangements, so there was plenty to do in addition to learning how to chant.

A Simcha More Than Four Decades in the Making was a wonderful experience in terms of both learning and celebrating. It's true, you know, that you can sing "Adon Olam" to just about any melody. In keeping with our 70s theme, our dear friend and cantorial soloist pored over lists of songs, experimenting with several until she landed on "I'd Like to Teach the World to Sing." It was perfect foreshadowing for that night's party which was complete with costumes and era-appropriate music. All had a groovy good time.

My quest to participate more fully in services has been fulfilled. I continue to challenge myself to truly read all parts of the service—even familiar portions—instead of just reciting them. And I'm always reminded of both the process and progress involved in those two years.

I didn't set out to become an adult Bat Mitzvah, but I'll forever be glad that I did.

Joan Bloomfield
Congregation Ohr Tzafon (Atascadero, California)

Judaism: A Journey from Childhood to Adulthood

Most girls of my generation didn't become Bat Mitzvah, especially growing up in a Conservative/Orthodox family. It never occurred to me to ask my parents about learning Hebrew in order to do this. Attending services as a child and adolescent wasn't something I really enjoyed, as they didn't touch my heart or spirit. It was the rituals and celebrating with my family that connected me to my Jewish faith. The lighting of the Shabbos candles on Friday night, the aromas of chicken soup, brisket and other special foods my mother prepared; these are memories that are still dear to me.

I also learned Yiddish from my grandma Anna, who was born in Russia/Poland. She spoke very little English, so I learned Yiddish at a young age listening to conversations between her and my mom. Sometimes after school I would walk over to her apartment in Brooklyn and help her with chores. I have a memory of watching her make blintzes from scratch. Around this same age, I began accordion lessons and I learned some Jewish music, such as "Sunrise, Sunset," "Exodus," and, of course, "Hava Nagila." Not only did my mother enjoy hearing this music, but there was also something special that stirred inside of me as I played these songs.

It was many years later, when I wanted to share my heritage with my five-year-old daughter Kami, that I began to study about the music and stories of the Jewish holidays and culture. Children's books were an easy resource for me to understand the history and customs of Judaism. Around 1985, I got a job teaching music and telling stories at Congregation Beth David's Torah School in San Luis Obispo. I also presented some programs about Jewish culture and traditions in Kami's elementary school classes. Later in the mid 1990s, when I became the children's librarian at the

Atascadero Library, I enjoyed presenting Jewish holiday programs at story time.

About 20 years ago, my mother had a friend from Brooklyn purchase a tallit (prayer shawl) for me as a gift. It meant a lot to me, even though I didn't know the meaning behind it. It wasn't until 2015 that I began to explore the possibility of becoming a Bat Mitzvah. I took Rabbi Janice's "Introduction to Judaism" and "Beginning Hebrew" classes. I learned that Judaism was a kaleidoscope of so many teachings—beginning with its complex history, celebrations, rituals, observances of Jewish dietary laws, love, marriage, and death. One of the most important Jewish missions is the concept of healing the world, known in Hebrew as *Tikkun Olam*. Rabbi Abraham Joshua Heschel wrote, "Remember that there is meaning beyond absurdity. Be sure that every deed counts, that every word has power, and that we all can do our share to redeem the world in spite of all absurdities, and all frustrations, and all disappointments. And, above all, remember to build a life as if it were a work of art." This is just as relevant today and speaks to me about some of the essence of Judaism.

Another experience that broadened my understanding of myself as a Jew was a trip to Israel in the fall of 1987. Eleven of us lived on an Army base outside of Tel Aviv and volunteered in a food factory for three weeks. I met my Israeli cousins and stayed with them one weekend. This trip opened my eyes to yet another aspect of Jewish identity; and that, along with Rabbi Janice's courses, inspired me to pursue a dream that I imagined for years—to become a Bat Mitzvah. Even though we are all a little older than 13, we four decided to go for it. And here we are today!

I'd like to share a quote from a favorite children's book called *Raisel's Riddle* by Erica Silverman: "It is written that learning is more precious than rubies, more lasting than gold. Rubies may be lost, and gold stolen, but that which you learn is yours forever." If we have a passion or a vision of learning or creating, then there's always a new adventure or journey waiting to be discovered. I have cherished this time to learn, grow, cry and laugh with these special friends—Frieda, Naomi and Mary. My study partner, Frieda, and I sometimes were ready to call it quits, but we kept going. Who knew Hebrew was harder to master than Spanish or French! It was a close match to giving birth! But after several months, with study and a few miracles, it all began to come together. Today would not have been possible without these women whom I call the "The Fearsome Foursome." I have been blessed to be a part of this greater Jewish community and supported by the loving members of the Congregation Ohr Tzafon family.

And of course, none of us could have succeeded without the encouragement, smiles and cheers from Rabbi Janice. Even though she earned a few more grey hairs from us, her teaching skills, discussions, creativity and enthusiasm took us on a wild ride and amazing journey. She helped to open doors that challenged us and gave us a better understanding and vision of ourselves as Jews.

I want to thank my friends, many of you who have made me a part of your family for 20-plus years. Thank you to my former library coworkers here today, who were my role models and gave me support and friendship over the years.

I want to thank my daughter Kami and her boyfriend, Jeremy, for flying in all the way from New Orleans to be here today. Kami, you have always been my pillar of support in my life's passions.

And finally, to my mom Irene, who I know is looking down from the heavens saying her famous phrase about my Bat Mitzvah: "I just can't believe it, this gives me chicken skin all over!"

Susan C. Levin
Congregation Gates of Prayer (Metairie, Louisiana)

I can truly say that preparing for and becoming Bat Mitzvah was one of the accomplishments of which I am most proud in my life. I was so happy to be given the opportunity by our wonderful educator at Congregation Gates of Prayer, Philip Gaethe. In the fall of 2003 he was offering an Intermediate Hebrew class which would culminate in an adult B-Mitzvah in spring of 2004.

I have always been a spiritual person, spending much time outdoors and enjoying nature as a child. My parents were very active in the Jewish community and taught religious school. My mother worked for the JCC for 17 years; my father, a professor at Tulane University, founded the Jewish studies program there. I have the fondest memories of visiting my Bubby and Zadie in Clarksdale, Mississippi and sitting next to my Bubby in the choir loft during Shabbat services. I've been singing in the Gates of Prayer volunteer choir now for over 25 years. And we would go visit my Nanny and Poppa in Nashville and eat kreplach soup and bagels and everything else Jewish that my Nanny would cook. We belonged to Touro Synagogue then, where Rabbi Leo Bergman boomed out his sermons on Civil Rights; and even though my childhood naïveté prevented me from comprehending what he was saying, I absorbed his gist. I have a strong yearning for social justice.

There was Jewish camp every summer, and then Touro Youth Group (SoFTY), and BBG. In my junior year of high school, I became the religious chairman of my chapter and enjoyed creating and organizing Shabbat services for my BBG sisters. In my mid-20s, I became a Friday night Shabbat service "regular" for life. Two years later, in 1980, I was catapulted spiritually by the illness and passing of my 49-year-old mom. During the six years she was ill, I had written poetry and read angel books. She had always told me that when someone dies, their soul goes back to G-d. I figured since G-d is everywhere, she could be as well. That is when I not only believed in G-d, but could FEEL G-d's presence, and knew then that G-d and my mother were with me all of the time.

We joined Gates of Prayer when my daughters were little girls. I was thrilled with Rabbi Bob Loewy, Cantorial Soloist Victoria May, and the worship services there. I threw myself into the volunteer life of this wonderful congregation, and taught first grade religious school for nine years. Gates of Prayer has been my second home. However, with all of the above, I never took the opportunity to learn Hebrew. I wanted to at least be able to follow along when Hebrew was read. I wanted to lead Shabbat services at the Jewish nursing home where I was working at the time. At that point, I felt it necessary to be validated in some way in order to do this, and making my Bat Mitzvah was the perfect opportunity. Moreover, since my husband had made his Bar Mitzvah when he was 13, and my two daughters had made their B'not Mitzvah, I was the lone one left in our family who had not.

I enjoyed my Hebrew class, as Phil is a fabulous teacher to students of all ages. He makes it really fun to learn! A few people dropped out of the class, and a married couple and I remained in order to make our B-Mitzvah. The final month before the B-Mitzvah, we were under the direction of Rabbi Loewy, another wonderfully animated and supportive educator.

I must say practicing every night was quite challenging and I had the most trouble with the Ma'ariv Aravim prayer, but I eventually got it! Every night I would sit at my desk and practice. And practice. And practice. My cockatiel Mango's cage was situated behind me on a cabinet. Following practice one night after I had just finished chanting my Torah portion, Mango began tweeting his own rendition of Ha'azinu! I just sat there listening to him with my mouth open. The next night I set out a tape recorder in hopes that he would do it again; unfortunately, he never did.

My younger daughter at the time was working at a dress shop

owned by a fellow congregant. I happened to be visiting one day and saw this shawl that I loved. I knew I wanted it for my Bat Mitzvah tallit and bought it. A friend of mine owned her own Judaica shop and she ordered the trim and tzitzit for me from New York. The shawl and trim then went back to the dress shop to be assembled. I got on the internet and found instructions on how to knot my own tzitzit. It was a sacred and spiritual task, as there are blessings to be said between each knot. I had just created my own Bat Mitzvah tallit!

It was such a memorable weekend! We led Friday night Shabbat services and I was honored to sing Debbie Friedman's "Ahavat Olam" by myself. The next day, the sanctuary was full of friends and family, and I couldn't believe the day had finally come. I stepped up to the bimah, and the words of Torah and Haftarah came alive, inhaled by my eyes and exhaled in the form of the beautiful melodies of the chants we all know and love. We all did a great job. All of that practicing had been worth it! My particular verses turned out to be the ones on animal sacrifice. Phil could not have given me a better section as I am an animal lover and animal rights activist. My D'var Torah was on how animals are sacrificed in today's world. It was exhilarating to be able to stand on "my" pulpit and preach about animal welfare! I was so proud to be a daughter of the commandments! A wonderful lunch ensued.

I will always cherish the beautiful memory of coming home afterward with my two daughters, 20 and 16 at the time. They were practically prancing while bringing the leftovers into the house; and we took some fun and silly pictures. I think they were really proud of me (sniff)! A few of my cousins had come in from Memphis, so Saturday night we all went out to eat and celebrate.

Because of what I had accomplished, my feelings of validation from making my Bat Mitzvah paved the way for many spiritual endeavors; and to this day I still lead services at the nursing home once a month, and at another once every two months. I love taking part in any service at Temple when asked. I now facilitate a guided meditation on Practicing Forgiveness every Yom Kippur afternoon; I also lead our Sisterhood Rosh Chodesh program. I firmly believe that making my Bat Mitzvah was my launching pad for taking advantage of these opportunities to share and teach Jewish spirituality. And, of course, I relish reading Hebrew, and whenever I do, the ancient letters light up, emanating and dancing on the pages of my Siddur.

Madelyn Carter Neufeld
Congregation Beth Chaim
(Princeton Junction, New Jersey)

I do not know that my journey to the Torah is all that extraordi-
nary. I grew up in Brooklyn, New York, the oldest daughter of two
Reform Jewish parents. To me, Judaism meant family and food.
Living in Brooklyn, I thought the entire world was Jewish. On
Rosh Hashanah, the world stopped: schools were closed; everyone
I knew hung out in front of the temple in their best clothing—a
place to be seen; the social event of the year. On Hanukkah, there
were menorahs in every window. Throughout elementary school we
had almost all Jewish students; only an occasional non-Jew. So, our
Jewish community was the community. There seemed no need to
go to temple or Hebrew school. I spent my life celebrating life cycle
events and holidays surrounded by a large, loud extended family,
gorging on my grandmother's glistening brisket and luchen kugel
with plump, dark raisins, and the ear-splitting banter of 10 aunts
and uncles and assorted cousins.

As the family grew smaller and I grew up, we moved from New
York to Maryland and I became acutely aware that the world was
not, in fact, all Jewish. Christmas trees filled each window; my
lonely menorah was one of just two on our entire street. Pregnant
with my first child, I felt the need to belong once again as I had
in Brooklyn. But I realized I would need to make an effort I never
before had to make. We joined a temple, sent our children to Jewish nursery school, and became active at the JCC. As my children
entered elementary school, I longed to go back home so they could
be with their grandparents, aunt and great grandmother. My family was rapidly shrinking and despite new friends in a new temple
family, I was feeling the need to be connected to more.

My husband and I decided to make the move back home after 11
years because we believed that family ties had to take precedence.

We moved close to my family, joined Congregation Beth Chaim and began again to make new connections. My husband joined the Men's Club and I the choir. The children went to Hebrew school and Camp Harlem and NYFTY where they have made lifelong friends. As I sang in choir each week during rehearsal and then at Friday night services and high holidays, I found the liturgy moved me in a way that I could not explain. The music filled my heart and soul with something deeper, something almost transformative. Although I had heard these tunes many times before as part of the larger congregation, singing them I felt lighter, calm, peaceful. Sitting on the bimah, the music washing over me, through me, brought me to a spiritual place I had not yet visited.

Having never learned Hebrew, and reciting the prayers for years by rote, I began to wonder what I was singing. Could the words I was reciting move me as deeply as the musical notes? What was the meaning behind each of the prayers? Could this new learning access a hidden spirituality deep within me? This love of the music and longing to understand led me to become a Bat Mitzvah in my mid 50s. Delving into the Torah, examining the words and meaning and exploring and dissecting the concepts with my fellow classmates, could only enhance what I might intuitively comprehend by the sound of the music alone. I wanted more, I needed more; perhaps this was the path.

Susan Rappaport
Temple Emanuel (Edison, New Jersey)

My Long-Delayed Bat Mitzvah

My mother always told me to wear my Jewish star necklace inside my shirt. She said, "The whole world needn't know you're Jewish."

When the holidays came around and both parents were working I often snuck into the children's services. Nobody noticed one extra kid.

When all the other neighbors and cousins went to Hebrew school I wanted to learn Hebrew too, but my mother said, "It's a waste of money."

When they all had B'nai Mitzvah, I attended theirs.

My mother lodged several complaints about anti-Semitism at her hospital job, and I remembered meeting her friend with the tattooed numbers on her arm.

My father spoke impeccable Yiddish and played the music constantly. But he believed in science and was not one to conform to nineteenth century rules.

Maybe it was when my father died and the torn black ribbon on my lapel echoed the tearing in my heart.

Maybe it was when my mother lay dying, and the hospice rabbi met us in the parking lot to sing the Mi Shebeirach.

Maybe it was after they found the tumor in my right breast, and I fervently prayed on the table as they kept re-scanning for bone metastasis.

Maybe it was when I got married for the first time at 59, and my husband stepped on the wine glass.

It could have been any of those moments; but somehow, I found myself sneaking back into the synagogue even though I was always afraid of doing the wrong thing, even though I felt like an outsider. Something in my bones craved that connection.

When a rabbi who I liked made me feel like I could belong and offered adult B'nai Mitzvah classes, I signed up.

It was not easy. I was uncomfortable. I struggled learning Hebrew. I struggled with the chanting, but I also enjoyed it.

I loved analyzing the text of the Torah. When I wrote my D'var Torah expressing my indignation over the Sotah portion, the rabbi encouraged all my questions.

On the day of the Bat Mitzvah as I stood on the bimah with three other women, I was not 13. But I was there.

All my family came. All my fears dissipated. My husband wrapped me in the tallit. I chanted without error.

I read my D'var Torah with all my feminist objections. The mystery from ignorance was gone. The mystery of religious meaning and profound traditions was here to stay.

I wear my Jewish star for all to see.

Suzanne Leichman
Temple Beth El (Tacoma, Washington)

Welcome, friends and family. My journey from conversion to my Bat Mitzvah has taken 45 years. During this time, I completed my Master of Arts in psychosocial nursing; raised two creative, genuine children; and had a satisfying career of public service—all with the support of my love and best friend, never-boring Howard of blessed memory.

My Torah portion concerns the building of the Tabernacle. It is instructive for the building of the structure, materials, and the sacred vestments. Design elements include gold, silver, and copper; blue, purple, and crimson yarns; goat's hair and fine linen; tanned ram skins; dolphin skins; acacia wood; oil for lighting; spices for the anointing oil and for the aromatic incense; lapis lazuli and other stones for setting. All of these elements are highly valued for their quality and beauty. The instructions include the whole community of the Israelites who excelled in ability as well as everyone whose spirit was moved to contribute. The portion is inclusive. It does not limit participants to those who are wealthy or part of the elite. It welcomes contributions from all. This is a lesson which is most important for us today. I believe that we enrich ourselves when we have diverse people in our lives. Our challenge as a nation, as a temple, and as individuals is to be inclusive. When you draw people around you, everyone benefits.

My tallit incorporates elements of my Torah portion into it: gold, silver, copper, blue, purple, and crimson yarns. Thank you, Shelley Rozen, for your skills and artistry.

My Torah portion is most fitting, because it references lifelong passions of art, fabric, and working with and encouraging people. I didn't choose my Torah portion; it chose me. It is the portion for my birthday week and is most appropriate.

When I was five my grandmother began teaching me to sew and

to embroider. I made doll clothes and then my own clothes. My mother offered to pay for fabric, patterns, and notions for any project as long as I completed one before moving on to the next. I saved scraps of fabric and began creating quilts. Then I acquired a variety of fabric for quilts. I love color and design and texture. When my energy is low, I visit fabric stores or spend time petting my fabric stash to replenish myself. Making friends and working with people has been central in my life. I love to hear people's stories and to help them on their journeys. The people in my life are the fibers, color, and texture which have made me who I am. Family and friends make the majority of my fabric. The many interesting and challenging patients and nursing students who shared their stories and allowed me to influence their lives have made the fabric of my life unique. My patients came from many backgrounds, but they shared one commonality—they were mentally ill. Working with them at times was draining. However, they gave me joy, especially when I could see that I was making a difference in the quality of their lives and they were learning from me.

I had many people helping me, from teachers to fellow students, who made me feel as if we were in this together. Thank you to Jeff Freedman, Deb Freedman, Karen Bloustein, and Stephanie Levine for helping me to learn Hebrew and to begin work toward my Bat Mitzvah. Rabbi Kadden, thank you for your support, understanding, and guidance. Thank you, again, to Shelley Rozen, who wove my beautiful tallit. Thank you to Cantor Beth Garden for making recordings for my study. Special thanks must go to Joan Garden who took me and my dyslexia on as a project. I know I have been a challenge. Thank you, Joan, for helping me to achieve this goal.

Leslie Rosenwasser
Temple Judea (Palm Beach Gardens, Florida)
In memory of my beloved grandmother Pauline Kirchner

The Long Journey Home, aka The Return of a Long-Lost Love
My very first memory of my Judaism is from around the age of five or six years old. Most weekends, my maternal grandmother would pick me up on Friday afternoon from my home and take me for the weekend to her home. My grandparents and I would return to my parents' home on Sunday at noon for a family dinner. On Friday afternoon, my grandmother would hand grind the chopped liver and then at dusk she would cover her head and light the candles, and my grandfather would recite—at breakneck speed—what I now know as the Kiddush.

The three of us would enjoy what I am sure was a wonderful roasted chicken dinner, but in truth all I remember is the grinder that was attached to the kitchen counter, the candles, and my grandfather and his incomprehensible words.

The next morning, my grandmother and I would get dressed up—this was the 1950s—and walk over to what seemed an enormous building. We would climb the stairs and I would look for my grandpa downstairs with all the other men.

In 1959, just nine days before my eighth birthday, my beloved grandmother died; and for many years after so did Shabbat for me.

Although my parents had both been raised in observant and kosher homes, there was only an inkling of their Jewish experiences visible in our home: a mezuzah on the front door, a Hanukkah menorah, and a Passover Seder led by my great uncle at a speed so fast and a language so foreign...we just hung out under the table.

The Catholic church has always said, "Give me a child for the first five years of their life and I will have them forever." I guess, luckily for me, that germ of Judaism that my maternal grandparents instilled in me lay dormant but alive—waiting for the nourishment of later life.

In 1961 or 1962, my parents joined a large Reform synagogue, Temple Beth-El, for the express purpose of preparing my brother for his Bar Mitzvah, which would occur in 1965. Theirs was a hands-off approach. Although we belonged to this vibrant community, I do not remember attending Shabbat services a single time as a child with my parents. There were no Friday night candles, no Kiddush, no roasted chicken dinners. Even when my brother became a Bar Mitzvah, my parents were not on the bimah. My grandfather had an aliyah. The emphasis was on the party and the clothing, and not on the significance of Jewish education.

When I told my parents that I was no longer interested in participating in Temple Beth-El events, Sunday school, Hebrew school and the like, there was no resistance. At the time, I was victorious in reclaiming my Sunday mornings and a couple of afternoons a week. It took many years to realize the opportunity I gave away.

I guess it was no surprise that I married a Gentile. He had stated that he did not care what religion our children would be, and we did not have a religious ceremony. We had two beautiful sons who were circumcised, but in the hospital environment. There was not even a discussion of a bris. We lived in rural southeastern Massachusetts, an enclave of former Puritans and present-day Catholics; hardly a Jew anywhere.

My Jewish practice was meager at best. We congregated as a family at my parents' home for a Seder, and there was always the menorah at Chanukah. But there was also a big shiny Christmas tree and no religious education for either of my boys. As the boys grew, a little voice within me began to feel uncomfortable with the holiday scenes. Passover remained intact, as did Chanukah, but there was no Shabbat and the Christmas tree really began to bother me. I tried to talk to my husband about a Jewish religious education for our sons, as I felt that they were going to grow up with absolutely no foundation. He told me flat out that he was not going to accept his sons being Jewish. Along with the other myriad problems that existed within our relationship, that was the last straw.

While my older son was lost to cultural Christianity and a marriage to a Gentile, he still looks forward to our annual Passover Seders. Any religion seems to be absent from his life.

My younger son is a different story entirely. Eric had always been asking about his Judaism. After our divorce, Eric eagerly studied Hebrew with a private teacher; and although he did not become a Bar Mitzvah, he was an active member of his confirmation class at our synagogues. Eric is a temple member and is happily married to a Jewish woman. My Passover this year was celebrated in their home, and everyone was there to celebrate.

Once I realized my failure of providing a Jewish education to my children, an interest in rekindling my Judaism was sparked. I joined temples in Hingham, Massachusetts and in Kalamazoo, Michigan; but other than attending High Holiday services, I never made temple participation a priority.

It was not until I moved to Tucson in 2003 that I began to change. Tucson seemed very foreign to me and my neighborhood was populated with very nice rednecks!! I went temple shopping to try and find some people like me! At least that is what I was thinking at the time. I still was without any religious Jewish background; I knew only the Sh'ma and the Chanukah blessing! I thought about what I could contribute to any synagogue and what I wanted from a synagogue. I was looking for friends and a place where I felt comfortable. In no time at all I was recruited to help run the sisterhood of a 750-family temple organization and the gift shop! The social part was great. I met loads of people, and many were even warm and friendly. As sisterhood president, I made it my business to attend Friday night services. I saw my role as an ambassador to new potential congregants. I was still without any religious roots. Week after week, the Shabbat service became familiar. I participated in the Hebrew marathon one weekend, but no class was offered in prayer book Hebrew. But repetition is a wonderful teaching tool, and soon things became more familiar. I struggled along on Friday nights with the transliteration and on the very few occasions when I was asked to recite a blessing, I had help from the internet.

When I moved to Florida in 2010 I knew that a priority for me was to find a synagogue. My first High Holidays, I tried Rosh Hashanah at Temple Beth Am. I was deeply disappointed. Ticket holders (as opposed to members,) were cordoned off in several rows in the back. The rabbi circulated throughout the congregation but did not come near to the ticket holder section. Not a single person said hello or wished me a Happy New Year. I never went back—not even for Yom Kippur, for which I had purchased a ticket. I was dismayed, and I was still not smart enough to realize that to know a congregation is to go for Shabbat.

My second attempt was at Temple Israel. The organization was run by its executive director. There was no contact at all with clergy. After doing a little research, I found out that the synagogue was in transition, and so I backed off. When I learned that they had recently hired a new rabbi in the summer of 2012 I bought tickets for "the holidays" and had a positive experience. I started going to Shabbat services. It was a small group on Friday nights—maybe 30 or so individuals. I volunteered to prepare their onegs and pronegs, and was an active participant for 1½ years in all things Temple Israel. I had developed a very close relationship with Rabbi Olshein. I attended numerous classes and Saturday morning Torah study sessions, and volunteered any time labor was needed. I was ready for more. I spoke to the rabbi. I wanted to study Hebrew; I wanted to be competent with the siddur. I needed to really understand the prayers and their meaning. Nothing happened. I spoke to the rabbi again and again. I sent emails. There was no response. None. I did not want to be a Jew without understanding the meaning of Jewish prayer and thought. I wanted to be competent.

Sadly, I realized that I needed to leave Temple Israel. I had come to realize that Temple Israel had become a place to go but without any real inner meaning. I wanted more.

An acquaintance had mentioned Temple Judea and I had attended a session at Temple Israel where Rabbi Yaron had participated. I liked his energy. I contacted Temple Judea. Amazingly, Rabbi Yaron got back to me. We engaged in a dialogue about me, about Temple Judea, what I could hope to get from this sacred place and what perhaps I had to offer. I met with Cantor Alicia. It was personal; I was touched, deeply. It was clearly worth a try. I would start with Shabbat and avail myself of whatever was being offered. At least that is what I thought. That plan was akin to drinking from a firehose: too much. I narrowed my focus and began to build a Jewish foundation for my own sake.

When I think of what the past year-and-a-half have brought me, I get goose bumps. I have grown and learned so much, not only about Judaism, but about myself as well.

My Bat Mitzvah and my Confirmation are just the beginning. Chanting Torah and Torah study are under my skin. There is so much to learn.

Nancy Barr, Wendy Bill, Sue Marcoe, Suzanne Neil, Roberta Schiff, Barbara Stapholz, Amy Thrasher
Congregation Shir Chadash (Freedom Plains, New York)

Why did seven busy and accomplished women work for over a year to be called to the Torah today? After all, in our tradition we attain the label of Bat Mitzvah upon the [nowadays] relatively effortless act of reaching our 13th birthday. The answers are as varied as our group: to meet the intellectual challenge of learning to read and chant Hebrew; to revisit a childhood experience with a deeper perspective; to improve our ability to participate in and understand the services we've attended much of our lives.

Our Torah portion, Behar, aptly speaks to the same themes of renewal, homecoming, and our responsibilities to our communities and the world at large.

We have found our study to be interesting and rewarding.

There are many people to thank for helping us reach this milestone, especially: the previous adult B-Mitzvah who inspired us; Jerry Scheck for his selfless gifts of time, patience and encouragement; our families and friends for their support of this long-term effort, Rabbi Daniel Polish for sharing his knowledge and wisdom; and Cantor Gail Hirschenfang for the love, talent, creativity and endless dedication she has brought to teaching us.

Sharon Roth
Temple Beth El (Great Neck, NY)

My name is Sharon. At the age of 52, I decided to try the B'nei Mitzvah course offered at Temple Beth El after several years of pondering the idea and finding every excuse not to do it.

I made my decision while my husband was traveling. The classes took place on Thursday evenings, a night that happened to fall either when my husband was out of town or at a business function. What did he have to do with all of this? I didn't want to tell him that I was taking this class because then he would insist that I finish it. I wanted to take this step to become closer to Judaism for me, not because someone else was putting pressure on me to do it.

I was born and raised outside of Los Angeles, in the Christian faith, and went to church often until the age of 15. I never questioned it, never challenged it, and never suspected that there may be other views. I was drawn to the security, stability, and structure of Christianity, and readily accepted the sermons each Sunday.

My mother died suddenly when I was 12, and my father died three years later. I was 15 when I became an orphan. I was shuffled from family member to family member, attending three different high schools in the tenth grade. I combined my junior and senior years, and graduated from high school a year early. I got married soon after high school graduation, upon turning 18. I was looking for security, stability, and structure.

I attended college at night while working full-time and graduated at the age of 24, shortly after my daughter was born. I got divorced a few years later, soon after my daughter turned three. As fate would have it, a year later I fell in love really for the first time, at the age of 27, with a man not only not of my faith but also not from Los Angeles. Not long after our relationship began, he wanted to move back to New York, and he wanted me to join him. We each had a precondition to our continued relationship: He would accept my daughter and I would convert to Judaism. So much for security, stability, and structure.

He held his end of the bargain unconditionally, with love, and his whole heart and soul. You could not ask for a better father.

I enrolled in conversion classes at Temple Emanuel in New York the Monday following my arrival. I went to the mikvah, was married by a rabbi, celebrated the Jewish holidays, prepared traditional holiday meals, raised "our" daughter in the Jewish faith, and celebrated a bris when our son was born several years later.

Although I may have accepted Judaism on the outside, I had not completely accepted Judaism on the inside. My lifelong beliefs were not washed away by the cleansing water of the mikvah. I did not understand the essence of being Jewish.

After our son's Bar Mitzvah four years ago, I became increasingly dissatisfied with my lack of knowledge and understanding of the Jewish faith. It was no longer enough for me to go to the High Holiday services and mimic what everyone else was doing. I wanted to begin a Bat Mitzvah program in the hope that I would find the connection I was looking for. I was tired of standing on the sidelines, yet I was fearful to take the next step. I was afraid of the time commitment, embarrassed to let people know how little I knew about my adopted faith, and absolutely petrified by the prospect of learning to read Hebrew.

Once the course started, I was intrigued by the different views introduced each week by my fellow students. I was intensely insecure about my lack of knowledge and understanding, and felt that I added little to the weekly group discussions. Having come from a faith where challenging what was read and questioning one's beliefs was not encouraged, I patiently waited for the rabbi to tell me what to believe. That did not happen. Instead, he turned the lessons around and asked what we believed and challenged us to look beyond the words on the page. With the warm encouragement of our group, I eventually found my own voice.

The first year was intellectually stimulating and engaging with no pressure. All we had to bring each week was the zeal to learn. The second year, however, was hard work. We began to focus on the service: learning to read Hebrew, researching our parshas, learning to read those portions from the Torah like any other 13-year-old boy or girl—but we were all well past 13!

While standing before the congregation the morning of my Bat Mitzvah, I felt for the first time the connection I was searching for. I was humbled by the power I felt coming from the Torah, and I was grateful that I finally felt part of the faith.

The two years I invested in training to become a Bat Mitzvah were liberating and empowering. In the process of learning more about Judaism, I learned more about myself, and the importance of overcoming fear in my life.

It's not just my belief in Judaism that has grown, but my belief in myself has allowed me to tackle new challenges. I would recommend it to any adult who wanted to become closer to the Jewish faith.

William Lehman
Temple Emanu-El, Birmingham Alabama

My Jewish Journey
(Read the day of his Bar Mitzvah ceremony on March 4, 2017)
Born and raised in Birmingham, I attended a private high school in Mountain Brook. My best friend was Jewish, as were many of my classmates. Because of my last name, *Lehman*, he assumed that I was Jewish. I am ashamed to say that because I valued our friendship, I never bothered to tell him that I was not. We talked about cars and girls and sports but never religion. I graduated with a diploma and a basic familiarity with the Jewish faith after four years of religion class.

Throughout my adult life—again because of my last name—in both professional and social settings, people would ask me if I was Jewish. My response was always the same: "Would it make any difference if I was?"—thinking that if these people were biased or prejudiced, maybe this was not a relationship that I wanted to be a part of. Later, some of these same people would come to me and say: "You're the only Jewish person I know" and then proceed to ask me about some Jewish custom, holiday, or ritual.

There is an old Jewish saying, at least I think it is Jewish, that the parent takes care of the child and then the child takes care of the parent. I took care of my elderly mother in her home for 20 years, managing her affairs with a durable power of attorney. When her health began to deteriorate, my attorney suggested that we petition the court for me to be appointed as her legal guardian so that I could make medical decisions for her that she could not or would not make for herself. The judge sent two court-appointed attorneys to the house to interview my mother to evaluate her state of mind and well-being and if she was happy with the quality of care that I was providing. I was not allowed to be present so as to ensure she would be candid and truthful in her responses. The last question one of the attorneys asked her was: "What is the ancestral origin of your married name?" My mother said: "Oh, it's Jewish, but I would die before I would ever tell my son that he has Jewish bloodlines and a Jewish heritage because his father had Jewish ancestors."

Reviewing the transcript of her interview, here was all the proof I needed and in the form of a court document! Fast forward to last year, I made my decision to convert to Judaism. After considerable self-reflection, research and study, I was ready to adopt the religion of my European Jewish ancestors.

I went to the Levite Jewish Community Center and walked up to the first person I saw who looked like they worked there and said: "I want to join." She said: "Fill out this application, name, address, phone, email and it's $74 dollars a month." "That's it?" I asked. "Yes" she responded. "No, no, you don't understand. I want to join the Jewish religion!" After she regained her composure, she listened patiently as I told her my story. And then she gave me Rabbi Miller's phone number and said, "Schedule a meeting with the rabbi. He will be able to help you. You're making the right decision!" Could I actually become Jewish someday?

Someday was starting to come together as I embarked on the formal conversion process, culminating in my conversion ceremony.

Thanks to the continuous encouragement and support throughout this process from Cantor Roskin, Rabbi Miller, Rabbi Haas and my temple family, I stand before you today with my fellow classmates as a candidate for Bar Mitzvah. For this is the adult equivalent of the Bar Mitzvah that I should have had some 50 years ago. So today, *someday* is finally here!!

***

Bar Mitzvah Torah Portion
(Presentation during the B'nei Mitzvah ceremony as part of the Shabbat service, Saturday, March 4, 2017)
Having heard several references to the original Indiana Jones

movie *Raiders of the Lost Ark*, maybe you remember Hollywood's depiction of what the Ark of the Covenant might have looked like. Our Torah portion is a blueprint design of and instructions for the construction of the Ark.

To summarize our Torah portions:

Lori's portion begins with the children of Israel being put on notice to prepare offerings of gold, silver and brass. Gloria's portion continues with offerings of fine linen and wool in colors of blue, scarlet and purple, animal skins dyed red, anointing oils and incense. Michelle's portion references precious stones for a breastplate and the design of a portable sanctuary or tabernacle, and furnishings to be described later for receiving these offerings.

Susan's portion describes the materials to be used for the Ark and its dimensions in cubits, the universal unit of measurement at that time. If you hold your arm out and up at a right angle at the elbow, a cubit is the distance from the tip of your middle finger to the bottom of your elbow, or approximately 18 inches.

My portion calls for golden rings to be fastened to each of the four corners of the Ark with long poles of Acacia wood passed through these rings—not to be removed so as to make it easier for the people to carry the Ark across the desert wilderness. Acacia wood is very similar to dogwood—hard, dense, and durable.

Linda's portion directs the people to place the testimony to be received inside the Ark and provides for a very ornate cover described in cubits and adorned with gold cherubim.

Jonathan's portion describes the cherubim and their placement on the cover in great detail with the Ark of the Covenant to be a vessel for the Testament. Jonathan reminds us in his words, and I'm quoting here:

> Just as the Ark of the Covenant is a vessel for the Testament, our bodies are vessels for the soul. Just as Hashem gives precise and intricate instructions for the making of the Ark, Hashem also creates our bodies according to a

magnificently detailed design. Just as Hashem spoke the words of Torah and makes them live, so did Hashem speak Creation into being, including all souls that stream from the one Soul. Just as the High Priest lifted the living Law from the Ark on Shabbat, and just as we, in our time, lift the scrolls from the Ark, so do we lift our hearts and soul to Hashem, acknowledging that our souls belong to Hashem. Each of us is an ark and the one Soul lives within each of us.

Speaking for my fellow classmates, we would like to thank Cantor Roskin for her tireless and tremendous efforts that began with our adult Hebrew class and continued up to today, making sure that we were all prepared to be called to the Torah as B'nei Mitzvah. We would like to thank Rabbi Miller, Rabbi Haas and our temple family for their continuous encouragement throughout our preparation. Last, we would like to thank our families and loved ones for their patience and support during all of the practice time required to make this day possible for all of us. And we invite you to join us after the service for an oneg in the atrium, sponsored by the 2017 B'nei Mitzvah Class.

SHABBAT SHALOM

And now, if y'all will indulge me for a brief moment, there's something that I would very much like to do —

(Turn and approach Linda still seated on the bimah, get down on one knee, open the ring box to reveal the ring) — "Linda, will you marry me?"

(Answer) "Absolutely!"

(Congregation now standing and shouting) — "Mazel Tov, Mazel Tov, Mazel Tov!"

(Note: Clergy, classmates and just about everyone else present—except Linda—knew I was going to ask her!)

My Journey to Adult Bat Mitzvah — Anonymous

My story began when I was born to an interfaith couple in the Midwest. My father was Jewish, and my mother came from a Lutheran family. They agreed to raise their children as Jews. I had a sister five years my senior, a twin brother, and a younger sister.

In my childhood I attended our temple's religious school, but my family was not very observant. Only three girls in our congregation had become B-Mitzvah. One of them was my older sister, and the other two were her classmates. None of the girls in my class were attending Hebrew School, only the boys. I have no memory of my brother studying Hebrew, or of a conversation with my parents, now of blessed memory, about him becoming Bar Mitzvah. While my brother and I were twins, obviously fraternal, we possessed vastly different skills and gifts. He was extremely mechanically inclined and gifted artistically; but he was dyslexic, and school was a struggle for him. I was his opposite, and we complemented each other. All these years I quietly assumed that the question of B-Mitzvah was never discussed because school was so difficult for my brother, and our parents, and none of the girls were going to Hebrew school anyway. I certainly did not expect to study Hebrew and Torah if my twin did not. I thought that would be humiliating for him. I did not blame him or my parents. That was just the way it was.

Fast forward 53 years. I had observed several adult B-Mitzvah ceremonies. I thought I might like to take that journey myself, but I was intimidated. When I had the opportunity to join an adult B-Mitzvah class, my thoughts returned to the question of how my "womb mate" would feel about that. I told him I was considering it and invited him to join me in the class. He respectfully declined. Having had an adult conversation with my brother, and the opportunity to be part of a class, I was ready, and this was my chance. I decided to go for it. As a dear friend, now of blessed memory, told me, "It's about time."

I was 66 years of age when I joined the adult B-Mitzvah class. I was one of a group of nine adults: two men and seven women. I was not the oldest, and far from the youngest. The opportunity came at a perfect time for me. I had just retired from a career as a nurse practitioner, and most of what I had been reading was professional literature to keep up with the required continuing education. I finally had time to pursue my other interests.

Our class met monthly as a group. We were given assigned reading and met individually with rabbis, the cantor, and the temple's educator as well. To a certain extent, study was also self-directed. I chose to study the tension between reason and custom, and found increased value in tradition, a better understanding of prayer, and a stronger connection to the Jewish people. We all participated in the service, read from the Torah, and wrote our own messages.

Contemplating writing about my experience, and having further conversations with my siblings about it, my older sister revealed to me that she had to plead with our parents to support her desire to become a Bat Mitzvah as her friends did. And my brother told me that he actually did attend Hebrew school, but only briefly because it was too difficult for him. I do not remember that at all. Where was I? Maybe we never talked about those things because I was a girl and a middle child. My younger sister never became Bat Mitzvah either. But times have changed, and attitudes about women are different. I forgive my parents for their part in our lack of communication, and I am sorry they were not with me to celebrate my *simcha*. I think they would have been pleased.

However bumpy my journey to become a Bat Mitzvah was, it was not as difficult as I thought it would be. Recognizing that my Bat Mitzvah was just the beginning of a longer journey, I know the process has enabled me to feel more self-confident and more connected to Reform Judaism and my congregation. I now need to learn more. I want to become more fluent in Hebrew and more learned. I want to be a better Jew.

ACKNOWLEDGEMENTS

Throughout my life, I have been blessed with knowing and encountering so many wonderful people whom I credit for helping me become the person I am today. First and foremost, I want to thank my husband Robert (aka Bobby Mac) for always being there for me and supporting every idea and desire I've ever had since we've met. I really couldn't have gotten this far without all your supportive words and constant cheering me on to become the writer I've always wanted to be. You have been my rock and support when I needed it and I truly value you as my life partner and am so grateful for the privilege of being your wife.

I would also like to thank my parents for providing me with an amazing private school education which I credit for my penchant for writing and my love of grammar and the written word. You have always encouraged me to be anything I've wanted to be, regardless of whatever silly idea I had in my head that I either gave up on or failed at completely. I very much appreciate the support you have given me throughout my life; and although I know my decisions and life path have not been easy for you, I know that no matter what, you will always be there for me and that means the world to me.

To my mother- and father-in-law, Helen and Jimmy, thank you so much for taking me in as your daughter and providing me with so much love and support in my life's journey. You have always encouraged me to keep trying, keep doing, and never give up. Your love and acceptance have always meant the world to me and I am so grateful for getting to be a part of your family. Thank you for everything you do and continue to do for Bobby and me.

To my cousins Tina and Victoria, and to my Aunt Rosann, thank you for always opening your home to me on Jewish holidays and Shabbat and providing me with multiple opportunities to use my love of Hebrew and Judaism to lead our family Seders every year.

I am very lucky to have cousins like you in my life. To John and Deborah, you have always been a valued part of our lives and have continued to be present at every simcha and celebration. Thank you for always being there and continuing to support me in my journey.

To my cousins Gracie and Albert, you two have always accepted me for the person I am and have been there for Bobby and me no matter what. I am truly grateful to have you in my life. Thank you so much for everything that you do. It truly means the world to me to know such amazing people.

To the amazing clergy that I hold near and dear: Rabbi Sarah Hronsky and Rabbi Eleanor Steinman of my synagogue, Temple Beth Hillel in Valley Village, California; and Rabbi Michael Mayersohn, Cantor Shana Leon, and Cantor Jen Roher—you have all been an influential part of my journey as a Jewish woman. Without you and your constant guidance and support, I would not be the person I am today. I thank you so much for everything you have taught me and for the incredible opportunity to learn everything it means to be Jewish. I know I have a long way to go.

I am truly grateful to know such amazing people. Thank you for everything you have done for me.

Thank you to all the wonderful former adult B-Mitzvah students from across the United States for sharing your Jewish journey with me as a contribution to this book. May your stories bring inspiration to readers from far and wide to take that next step and begin their own Jewish journeys that will one day lead them to become a B-Mitzvah. You all are an inspiration and I hope you will continue on your path to bring your knowledge and passion to those around you.

Lastly, I am deeply grateful to the clergy, staff, and community at Temple Judea for being our family's spiritual home and a source of strength, guidance, and belonging. We look forward to many happy memories to be made there in the future.

TODA RABA!

GLOSSARY

Aleph Bet: The Hebrew alphabet

Aliyah: Honor of reciting blessings over the Torah. Meaning "ascent," refers both to the physical ascent onto the platform where the Torah is read and to the spiritual elevation experienced at that time.

B-Mitzvah/B'nai Mitzvah/B'nei Mitzvah: Children of the Commandment (We use B-Mitzvah throughout the book to keep things simple.)

Bar: Son

Bat: Daughter

Bimah: The podium or platform in a synagogue from which the Torah is read.

B'not: Daughters

D'var Torah: A talk on topics relating to a parashah (section) of the Torah.

Kippah (also, yarmulke): A small circular cap that is placed on one's head as a sign of reverence for G-d. In more liberal movements, a kippah is worn by both men and women alike and is predominantly worn during religious services. In conservative and Orthodox movements, only men wear kippot, and at all times (with the exception of sleeping and bathing).

Kippot: Plural of Kippah

Kol: All or any

Mazel Tov!: A Hebrew phrase expressing congratulations or wishing someone good luck.

Mikvah: A ritual bath filled with naturally occurring, free flowing waters that symbolizes cleansing, rebirth, and renewal.

Minyan: A group of 10 or more Jews over the age of 13; required for traditional Jewish communal worship.

Mishkan Tefilah: Hebrew for "Dwelling Place for Prayer." Also the title of a prayer book prepared for Reform Jewish congregations around the world by the Central Conference of American Rabbis (CCAR).

Mishnah: Part of the Talmud, the Mishnah contains detailed discussions of halacha, or Jewish law.

Parashot: Plural of Parashah

Parashah: A section the Torah

Pesach: Hebrew for Passover

Shalom: Hebrew for Peace

Siddur (pl., siddurim): Jewish prayer book, containing a set order of daily prayers

Tallit (pl., tallitot): Sometimes written tallis. A long rectangular shawl with four corners, each containing strings tied with knots known as *tzitzit*, which represent the 613 commandments in the Torah.

Tallitot: Plural of Tallit

Tanakh:A Hebrew acronym encompassing the canonical collection of Jewish texts. It contains Torah, Nevi'im (Prophets), and Kethuvim (Writings).

Torah: The scroll containing the Five Books of Moses

Trope: Cantillation. This is the distinctive melodic system used to chant Torah. Markings on each word indicate the melody to use to chant that word. It's a sort of musical shorthand.

Tzitzit: Fringes attached to the corners of garments as a reminder of the commandments; found on the corners of tallitot. The numerical value of the word *tzitzit* is 600. Each tzitzit has 8 threads and 5 knots which make a grand total of 613:which corresponds to the 613 commandments of the Torah.

Yad (lit., hand; pl., yadayim): A pointer used when chanting from the Torah to hold one's place, and so that our hands do not touch the scroll.

Yarmulke (also, kippah): A small circular cap that is placed on one's head as a sign of reverence for G-d. In more liberal movements, a yarmulke is worn by both men and women alike and is predominantly worn during religious services. In Conservative and Orthodox movements, only men wear a yarmulke, and at all times (with the exception of sleeping and bathing).

Yasher Koach!: Hebrew for *May You Have Strength!*

RESOURCES

Below is a list of some helpful resources I used while undergoing the journey to my Bat Mitzvah. This is only a sampling of all the information that is out there and available to you during your journey. Your clergy can also provide you with other materials and information that will prove tremendously helpful in your coursework.

Books

Living a Jewish Life, Anita Diamant

The Complete Idiot's Guide to Understanding Judaism, Rabbi Benjamin Blech

Jewtopia: The Chosen Book for the Chosen People, Bryan Fogel and Sam Wolfson

Born to Kvetch: Yiddish Language and Culture in all of Its Moods, Michael Wex

The Modern Jewish Girl's Guide to Guilt, Ruth Andrew Ellenson

Jewish with Feeling: A Guide to Meaningful Jewish Practice Rabbi Zalman Schachter-Shalomi with Joel Segel

Essential Judaism: A Complete Guide to Beliefs, Customs & Rituals, George Robinson

Websites

Reform Judaism: reformjudaism.org

United Synagogue of Conservative Judaism: uscj.org
Chabad: chabad.org
The Jewish Federations of North America. Find your local Federation chapter here: jewishfederations.org
American Jewish University: aju.edu

YouTube Videos for Learning

Tricks of the Trope by Hazzan Arianne Brown
Basic Trope Combinations by Michael Weis
Aleph Bet by Debbie Friedman
Torah Aliyah Blessings by Siddur Audio

Mikvah Resources

What is a Mikvah? Introduction to the Jewish Ritual Bath: bimbam.com/mikvah/
Mikvah Information: mikvah.org

About the Author

Christine Machlin is a Jewish writer whose passion for storytelling is deeply rooted in faith and self-discovery. She proudly celebrated her Bat Mitzvah in her 30s, an experience that transformed her spiritual journey and strengthened her connection to Judaism.

She believes it's never too late to embrace your faith or rediscover who you are, and encourages anyone thinking about taking this meaningful step to go for it with an open heart.

Recent books from *Ben Yehuda Press*

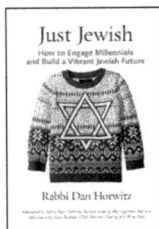

Just Jewish: How to Engage Millennials and Build a Vibrant Jewish Future by Rabbi Dan Horwitz. Drawing on his experience launching The Well, an inclusive Jewish community for young adults in Metro Detroit, Rabbi Horwitz shares proven techniques ready to be adopted by the Jewish world's myriad organizations, touching on everything from branding to fundraising to programmatic approaches to relationship development, and more. "This book will shape the conversation as to how we think about the Jewish future." —Rabbi Elliot Cosgrove, editor, *Jewish Theology in Our Time*.

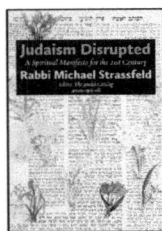

Judaism Disrupted: A Spiritual Manifesto for the 21st Century by Rabbi Michael Strassfeld. "I can't remember the last time I felt pulled to underline a book constantly as I was reading it, but *Judaism Disrupted* is exactly that intellectual, spiritual and personal adventure. You will find yourself nodding, wrestling, and hoping to hold on to so many of its ideas and challenges. Rabbi Strassfeld reframes a Torah that demands breakage, reimagination, and ownership." —Abigail Pogrebin, author, *My Jewish Year: 18 Holidays, One Wondering Jew*

A Passionate Pacifist: Essential Writings of Aaron Samuel Tamares. Translated and edited by Rabbi Everett Gendler. Rabbi Aaron Samuel Tamares (1869-1931) addresses the timeless issues of ethics, morality, communal morale, and Judaism in relation to the world at large in these essays and sermons, written in Hebrew between 1904 and 1931. "For those who seek a Torah of compassion and pacifism, a Judaism not tied to 19th century political nationalism, and a vision of Jewish spirituality outside of political thinking this book will be essential." —Rabbi Dr. Alan Brill, author, *Thinking God: The Mysticism of Rabbi Zadok of Lublin*.

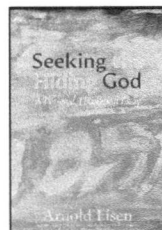

Seeking the Hiding God: A Personal Theological Essay by Arnold Eisen. "This generation's preeminent scholar of contemporary Jewry, Arnold Eisen has devoted his career to studying the spiritual strivings within the Jewish soul. In *Seeking the Hiding God*, Eisen provides a personal window into his own theological vision. Eisen's explorations will inspire readers to ask today's urgent questions of meaning and faith." —Rabbi Dr. Elliot Cosgrove, author of *For Such a Time as This: On Being Jewish Today*.

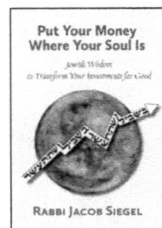

Embracing Auschwitz: Forging a Vibrant, Life-Affirming Judaism that Takes the Holocaust Seriously by Rabbi Joshua Hammerman.The Judaism of Sinai and the Judaism of Auschwitz are merging, resulting in new visions of Judaism that are only beginning to take shape. "Should be read by every Jew who cares about Judaism." —Rabbi Dr. Irving "Yitz" Greenberg

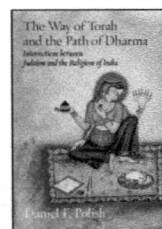

Put Your Money Where Your Soul Is: Jewish Wisdom to Transform Your Investment for Good by Rabbi Jacob Siegel. "An intellectual delight. It offers a cornucopia of good ideas, institutions, and advisers. These can ease the transition for institutions and individuals from pure profit nature investing to deploying one's capital to repair the world, lift up the poor, and aid the needy and vulnerable. The sources alone—ranging from the Bible, Talmud, and codes to contemporary economics and sophisticated financial reporting—are worth the price of admission." —Rabbi Irving "Yitz" Greenberg

The Way of Torah and the Path of Dharma: Intersections between Judaism and the Religions of India by Rabbi Daniel Polish. "A whirlwind religious tourist visit to the diversity of Indian religions: Sikh, Jain, Buddhist, and Hindu, led by an experienced congregational rabbi with much experience in interfaith and in teaching world religions." —Rabbi Alan Brill, author of *Rabbi on the Ganges: A Jewish Hindu-Encounter*.

Recent books from *Ben Yehuda Press*

Burning Psalms: Confronting Adonai after Auschwitz by Menachem Rosensaft. "It's amazing that Menachem Z. Roser saft's *Burning Psalms: Confronting Adonai after Auschwitz* doesn't burst into flames. This book of poetry — every poem in it a response or counterpoint to every one of the psalms in the biblical book — written by the son of Holocaust survivors and the brother of a murdered sibling he never knew, is composed with fire, fueled by a combination of rage, love, and despite-it-all faith that sears your eyes as you read it." —*New Jersey Jewish Standard*

Weaving Prayer: An Analytical and Spiritual Commentary on the Jewish Prayer Book by Rabbi Jeffrey Hoffman. "This engaging and erudite volume transforms the prayer experience. Not only is it of considerable intellectual interest to learn the history of prayers—how, when, and why they were composed—but this new knowledge will significantly help a person pray with intention (*kavanah*). I plan to keep this volume right next to my siddur." —Rabbi Judith Hauptman, author of *Rereading the Rabbis: A Woman's Voice.*

Blessed Are You, Wondrous Universe: A Siddur for Seekers. Non-theistic Jewish prayers by Herbert J. Levine. "Herb Levine has fashioned a sparkling collection of prayers for a thinking, feeling modern person who wants to express gratitude for the wonder of existence." —Daniel Matt, author, *The Essential Kabbalah*. "An exercise in holy audacity." —Dr. Shaul Magid author, *The Necessity of Exile*

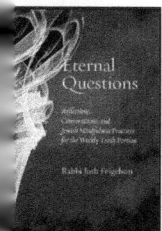

Siddur HaKohanot: A Hebrew Priestess Prayerbook by Jill Hammer and Taya Shere. Creative and traditional Jewish rituals and prayers that explore an earth-honoring, feminine-honoring spirituality with deep roots in Jewish tradition. "Far more than a prayerbook, this is a paradigm-shifting guidebook that radically expands our religious language, empowering us to reclaim what our souls have known for centuries: how to cook, season, and feast on our love of life, Spirit, and each other." —Rabbi Tirzah Firestone, author, *The Receiving: Reclaiming Jewish Women's Wisdom*

Eternal Questions by Rabbi Josh Feigelson. These essays on the weekly Torah portion guide readers on a journey that weaves together Torah, Talmud, Hasidic masters, and a diverse array of writers, poets, musicians, and thinkers. Each essay includes questions for reflection and suggestions for practices to help turn study into more mindful, intentional living. "This is the wisdom that we always need—but maybe particularly now, more than ever, during these turbulent times." —Rabbi Danya Ruttenberg, author, *On Repentance and Repair.*

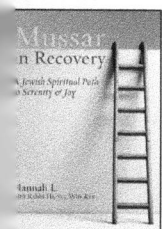

Mussar in Recovery: A Jewish Spiritual Path to Serenity & Joy by Hannah L. with Rabbi Harvey Winokur. "A process of recovery that is physically healing, morally redemptive, and spiritually transformative." —Rabbi Rami Shapiro, author of *Recovery: The Twelve Steps as Spiritual Practice*. "A lucid and practical guidebook to recovery." —Dr. Alan Morinis, author, *Everyday Holiness: The Jewish Spiritual Path of Mussar.*

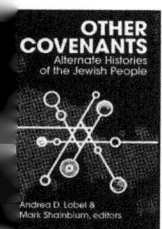

Other Covenants: Alternate Histories of the Jewish People by Rabbi Andrea D. Lobel & Mark Shainblum. In *Other Covenants*, you'll meet Israeli astronauts trying to save a doomed space shuttle, a Jewish community's faith challenged by the unstoppable return of their own undead, a Jewish science fiction writer in a world of Zeppelins and magic, an adult Anne Frank, an entire genre of Jewish martial arts movies, a Nazi dystopia where Judaism refuses to die, and many more. Nominated for two Sidewise Awards for Alternate History.